IN THE WAITING

THE JOURNEY BETWEEN THE WILDERNESS AND THE PROMISED LAND

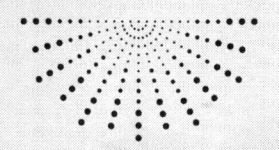

CHER BUTLER
POEMS: RUTHIE DICKEY

Cover & Artwork:
JEFFREY LIU

I WILL NOT KEEP SILENT MINISTRIES, INC.

Cher Butler

I Will Not Keep Silent Ministries, Inc.

Iwnks.com

ISBN: 9798871545461

DEDICATION

I dedicate this book to a teacher at Windsor Elementary who said to me, "Sign this piece of paper."
"Why?" I asked.
She answered, "So that I can have your autograph when you write your first book."
I don't remember your name, but I want to thank you for prophesying this into my life. I hope God gets this book into your hands.

CONTENTS

INTRODUCTION

When we receive Christ, we embark on a journey from the wilderness to the promised land. On a journey from the places of our brokenness into *the more* of God. On it, we become the people we need to be in order to walk out the call God's given us. So often, people get saved and want to instantly jump into ministry without realizing that every general of the faith has walked a journey of waiting in which God prepared them for their call. Every general has experienced a period or process before their promises from God came into fruition. The Israelites waited forty years in the wilderness because they complained and didn't trust God. Some of us will have long waiting periods, as God works out His healing and purification in our lives before launching us into our destiny.

The journey from the wilderness is not instant, but progressive. But the wait is worth it, because when we get there, we will have the character, purity, and healing needed to fulfill our call. In the chapters of this book, aside from my childhood, I have laid out the elements of God's work in my life over the last seven years of my relationship with Him—what I call *the waiting*—in hopes that it will help and inspire your own journey toward *the more* of God and His call for your life.

The first half of the book highlights the Christian journey out of the wilderness—the journey of salvation, healing, and deliverance. When we first come to Him, we have a lot to sort through and be purified from, but too many people stop with their conversion and miss out on the fullness of all God has for them. The waiting begins with a call from God. This calling predated my salvation experience and led me to eventually receive Christ. After that, God brought me into the refiner's fire where I experienced His purification process and began to receive healing in my heart. Then, I entered a season of divine revelation in which I began to experience the power of the Holy Spirit and the "unsearchable things" of God. After this, I experienced a stripping away, a pruning process, and a wilderness season in which God removed unhelpful things from my life and taught me to discern between His thoughts and the lies of the enemy. This led into a dynamic experience of inner healing and deliverance that ultimately launched me into my ministry calling.

The second half of the book highlights the continued journey toward the promised land, the journey of maturation and purification. After I stepped into ministry, God still needed to bring increased maturity and growth. I also began to learn about prophetic puzzles and how pivotal times in our lives form our destiny in God. After this, God took me into a season of revealing in which He exposed even deeper layers of my heart and brought greater purification through obedience. He also invited me into deeper levels of intimacy with Him, which prepared me to step more fully into His calling for my life. As part of my preparation process, God also taught me how to walk in the fruit of His Spirit and to overcome the trials that come. After that, God began to speak to me about the current state of the church and His will for His church to rise and shine for His kingdom. Most importantly, during *the waiting*, I discovered how to walk in true friendship with God, which is the foundation for everything else. I pray this book blesses you and illuminates your own journey from the wilderness into the promised land and *the more* of God.

POEM: THE CALLING

I hear your voice.
I see your face.
You call my name.
You dwell within me.
Your whispers ring loud and clear.
You call me to the mountains.
On high, you gather your eagles.
The time is now.

Your spirit cries out for the remnant.
Rise up, dear children, for the time is now.
Can you hear the eagles call?
Arise, arise, you appointed ones.
Seers, look and see what the Lord is doing.
A new calling is at hand.
Rise above the fray.
Look and see that the Lord is good.

—Ruthie Dickey
Vice-President, I Will Not Keep Silent Ministries

1

THE CALL

For many are called, but few are chosen (Matthew 22:14).

Life in Christ begins with His call. You have been called. You are being called right now. Don't ignore the invitation. Save the date, for today is the day of salvation. And for those who are already saved, today is the day of divine revelation. Today is the day when the more of God floods into your life.

In Matthew 22:1–14, God paints a picture of a beautiful wedding feast for His son, Jesus Christ. He first invited the religious leaders, but they rejected His call. Then, He asked the Jews, His people, but they also declined His invitation. Last, He invited everyone else, and from that group, some finally answered the call. Yet at the wedding feast, one man came dressed inappropriately for the occasion. His poor attire reflected the condition of his heart, showing that his heart was not for God. We must give our hearts to God and answer the call. All of heaven is calling you. If you haven't yet, will you respond?

I first received God's invitation many years ago. Looking back on my prophetic timeline, I can pinpoint when I received the invitation from God to come to His wedding feast and meet His son. God had woven His supernatural calling throughout my life up to that particular moment in time. Suddenly, veils began falling from my eyes, and I could see the pattern, the prophetic puzzle of His love in my life, as some pieces came together. The calling of Jesus was like an infusion of love injected into my spirit, soul, and body producing unwavering hope, which has lingered through my life. As I take you on this journey, sharing how God called me and saved me, the other prophetic puzzle pieces will come together.

For so long, the puzzle pieces of my childhood were scattered all over the place, and I didn't know how to fit them together. I had significant lapses in my memory caused by my mind's efforts to block out trauma so that I could survive. For so long, I couldn't remember parts of my childhood. It appeared only as blurred memories of light and darkness dominated by fear and demons and accompanied by a chaotic mix of love, hate, extreme pain, sadness, joy, and disappointment. Yet I also felt hope. As I dig through all the rubbish, I can pull out golden moments buried in the mix. It's a precious memory; one I'll never forget. When I was fourteen, I felt the love of God so strongly when my grandpa, Kenneth Randall, died. God's love entered the hospital room, and I knew God was among us in that place.

MY EARLY CHRISTIAN UPBRINGING

I had been raised in what appeared to be the perfect little Christian church in a small town on a quiet neighborhood street. People peacefully walked their dogs down the road, children laughed and played in the front yards, and all seemed well in the world. Each Sunday, I learned all the Christian phrases and appropriate conduct. I learned about religious tradition, I memorized Bible verses, and I saw a lot of fake smiles. Later, I realized that a pattern of witchcraft and control lurked behind the Christian phrases, keeping people in bondage while desperately trying to maintain a persona. Behind all the religious traditions, ugly demons produced spiritual pride and quenched the move of the Holy Spirit. I memorized verses in the Bible as I was taught and as a sign of good works, but I lacked revelation and knew nothing of the Holy Spirit. Behind all the fake smiles, souls begged for deliverance and healing, but never received anything. Instead, they continued to waste away.

Unfortunately, this sounds familiar to too many people. We should get healed, saved, and delivered when we go to church, but sadly, many do not. If this resonates with you and you need help in your life today, great hope awaits you—the hope of Jesus. Maybe you feel like you've heard all the teachings, but you don't know the man. If you want to know Jesus' nature, dive into the scriptures for yourself. Don't just listen to what others say. Go and look for yourself. Let this scripture give you a glimpse of His nature.

Bless and affectionately praise the Lord, O my soul, and do not forget any of His benefits; who forgives all your sins, who heals all your diseases; who redeems your life from the pit, who crowns you [lavishly] with lovingkindness and tender mercy; who satisfies your years with good things, so that your youth is renewed like the [soaring] eagle (Psalms 103:2–5 AMP).

The name of Jesus Christ is power. Not only that, but the name of Jesus also bears a light source of authority and is dominating. One thing I did receive from the church was the light source of His name, which penetrated deep within my spirit, leaving a tiny, holy spark of His calling. I knew then that I loved Jesus, but I often wondered if He loved me back and if this call meant anything. I knew there was something more, yet I felt confused and tormented by pain, stricken by my early years of abandonment, foster care, and adoption. The enemy loved screaming *victim* into my soul, and I bought the lie for a while. The noise inside my head was too loud; I couldn't keep following the call. It seemed like it gently faded away, and I began to swim in a sea of nothingness named hopeless despair. *Why, oh God, have You forsaken me?* I thought. I built up walls and made inner vows to protect my heart, and in doing so, I created a theology that permitted me to continue to do what was right in my own eyes. Have you ever made up your own Jesus? You know, the Jesus who conforms to you, but you don't conform to Him or His word?

As time trickled on, I followed the dark trail of my ancestors and biological family by opening many doors to the devil and his demons. Some doors were opened to me while in my mother's womb. Yes, the womb is an open door. David spoke of this concept in Psalms 51:5, which reads, *"Behold, I was brought forth in iniquity, and in sin did my mother conceive me."* As I followed a road of destruction, at the same time, God's little fireballs of glory encountered me along the way, luring me back to Him and my calling.

My adopted mom became one of the biggest blessings during this time as she graciously taught me about Jesus while suffering through her own physical sickness and spiritual battles. However, a mother's love just wasn't enough for me; I had to find my own way while in my state of rebellion. In short, I had to find myself. Between the ages of fourteen and nineteen, I opened doors to drugs, alcohol, sex, vanity, and many other destructive behaviors. But I did find myself, finally. I found myself at the end of a rope that led to utter darkness, where suicide seemed like a good option for the redemption of my pain. At the end of ourselves is a body made of dust, but if we allow God in, He will infuse our vessel of dust with His glory. Death leads us to dust, but God leads us to glory. His glory is who He is and His manifest presence in us. As Paul the apostle wrote:

To them God chose to make known how great among the Gentiles are the riches of the glory of this mystery, which is Christ in you, the hope of glory (Colossians 1:27 ESV).

THE DAY OF SALVATION IS TODAY

I'll never forget the day I first stepped toward God's glory. I was nineteen and living with my grandma, who I loved dearly. As I lay in bed, wide awake and staring into the darkness of the room, which mimicked the darkness of my heart, I felt the nudge to call out to the one who had called me first. I said, *"God if You are real, show Yourself to me. I need You, and I'm sorry for everything. Help me."* After that prayer, the rest is history. By history, I mean, His-story. My story is a story of true redemption, a story of being called into something so great, vast, and unknown that I couldn't have imagined it in my wildest dreams.

Not long after I prayed that prayer, the dreams started. Wild dreams from God, so to speak. A few nights later, I prayed about something and received the answer to my prayer in a dream—in a Bible verse written across a windowsill. I woke up almost forgetting what had happened in the dream realm, but suddenly, it came into my mind like a rocket, and wonder filled my soul and spirit. I thought, *Oh, I have to search out this great King who is speaking directly to me.*

THE MYSTERIOUS PURSUIT OF GOD

The pursuit was on. I was ready to uncover the mysteries swirling in the atmosphere as I felt His calling intensifying. It was almost like He had tied a string around my heart and was pulling me close. It felt so mysterious, exciting, and even scary at times. I know this was the fear of the Lord, which soon overtook the demonic fear that, until that point, had plagued me all my life. I read through the New Testament repeatedly, utterly astonished at what I read. I felt like I was meeting the Lord in a new way I'd never heard of because the churches I had attended kept it either religious or surface level. Religious churches are dull and void of God's power, but invite man-made structures. Surface-level churches are often called "seeker-friendly;" they get people in the door, but never take them fully in to Jesus.

I did not understand this new level of faith, hope, and love, but I could not get enough of it. *What is this power I have never seen or heard?* I wondered. I felt like a little girl unwrapping a gift on Christmas morning. It was so exciting, but at the same time, I thought, *Why didn't anyone give me this gift earlier?* Now I know it's because no human can give you this gift. Only God can. The key is to search as soon as you hear the call. You will read this book and know this is for you, but what will you do about it? Jesus told us what to do:

Ask, and it will be given to you; seek, and you will find; knock, and it will be opened to you. For everyone who asks receives, and the one who seeks finds, and to the one who knocks it will be opened (Matthew 7:7–8 ESV).

When you knock, you're knocking on the door, which is Jesus:

"I am the door. If anyone enters by me, he will be saved and will go in and out and find pasture" (John 10:9 ESV).

And when you enter, you're going into the secret place under the shadow of the Almighty. As the psalmist wrote: *"He who dwells in the shelter of the Most High will abide in the shadow of the Almighty"* (Psalms 91:1 ESV).

Jesus' supernatural call persuaded me into the love chamber. His persistent pursuit—loving me first and calling my name into the darkness—opened my heart to Him. I felt like He was inviting me to sit down and stay awhile. However, when I sat, I saw so many unknowns. I couldn't see past the vast darkness, but I called out, *"Show Yourself to me,"* and I began to see the treasures He had for me. Walking on the pathway with Jesus, throughout the journey, I began to see the intangible treasures of the heavenly realm become tangible in my life. We will uncover these treasures throughout the timeline of this book. My hope is that you will start to remember the treasures God has placed in your life as well. Even through all the darkness of life, He always shines His light on us, but we so often overlook it.

Instead of seeing and writing about the doom and gloom of life through the lens of our earthly eyes, I am focusing on life through the lens of my spiritual eyes, which God has enlightened to enable me to see the good and pure. You too can learn to see with spiritual eyes. Below, I have included a prayer to have your spiritual eyes opened. Pray it, and then brace yourself, because you will start seeing like never before. This prayer comes straight from scripture, and you can insert yourself directly into the prayer to unlock all that God has for you (see brackets).

Dear Lord, I pray that the God of our Lord Jesus Christ, the Father of glory, may give to you [me] a spirit of wisdom and revelation in the knowledge of Him. I pray that the eyes of your [my] heart may be enlightened, so that you [I] will know what is the hope of His calling, what are the riches of the glory of His inheritance in the saints, and what is the surpassing greatness of His power toward us who believe. These are in accordance with the working of the strength of His might, which He brought about in Christ when He raised Him from the dead, and seated Him at His right hand in the heavenly places, far above all rule and authority and power and dominion, and every name that is named, not only in this age but also in the one to come. And He put all things in subjection under His feet, and gave Him as head over all things to the church, which is His body, the fullness of Him who fills all in all. Amen (see Ephesians 1:17–23 NASB1995).

This prayer is mighty because it is aligned with God's will, which is revealed in His word. You don't have to understand everything in this prayer right away. Understanding will come along the way. Just know that as you pray it, you are aligning with God's will for your life, and good things will start to happen.

As I continued to read through the scriptures about Jesus, my heart burned with holy fire. I literally had to see Jesus. I needed to know—*Where are You? Where is Your power? Who are You, really?* The questions just kept coming. I felt so alive. My call was activated, and I was His, even though I didn't know what any of that meant. I didn't even understand the scriptures yet, but I knew I had to tell everyone about the *treasure* I had found. I had finally found the love my heart had desired. God had instantly made me whole in spirit and saved me from myself as I ascended into the holy place with God—the secret place of His presence.

When I was born of water and Spirit and then joined to the Lord, my identity was sealed in Him. However, it took me years to understand this supernatural mystery. For me, getting saved wasn't a scripted prayer. It was more like a hand held out to me, while I struggled in the depths of crippling waves, and pulling me into another realm, the realm of the Spirit. When this happened, in a moment, I was reborn. In this place, I found a love strong enough to break down the barrier of my human mind, and I met the King who was and is and is yet to come (see Revelations 1:8). The same can be true for you. If what you're doing isn't working, grab the hand in front of you and speak with your heart. At that moment, you will align with heaven. Today is the day of salvation; don't delay.

Not too long before my salvation, I had prayed a simple prayer saying, "Dear Jesus, I pray that not one day goes by when I don't think of You." Previously, I would fill the voids and drown the pain inside me with things the enemy handed me on a silver platter. It seemed right then, because I lived by the motto, "Do whatever feels good and makes you happy." Soon, however, I discovered that those words are the main motto in the satanic Bible. With all the effort I put into pleasing my flesh in hopes of healing my soul, I often forgot about the small fire in my heart for Jesus. One day I woke up and realized it had been a while since I had even thought of Him, and I didn't like that.

Little did I know that God had heard that prayer and turned it into an overflowing river. I became the Jesus freak or the radical who never stopped talking about Him. I didn't know much of anything, but I knew His love and salvation, so I shared it with everyone. The more I read about Him, the more questions I had. I was in awe and wonder. I thought, *Why aren't we seeing the same miracles Jesus performed? Didn't He say we would do even greater works? I don't even see the smallest of works.* All I had ever heard were religious sermons with fancy wording about a Jesus who loves all of us no matter what. I couldn't stop wondering, *Why haven't I seen any miracles?* My heart yearned to know about the miracles. Since then, I have realized that working miracles is part of my calling. It wasn't long before God began to answer my hunger for miracles.

In fact, my hunger aligned with His desires in a way that released something supernatural. See, God speaks faster than thought; it's an instant knowing in which God converses with an individual almost at the speed of light. We can have whole books or innovative ideas downloaded into our minds in a mere second. This can happen instantly, or over time as we commune in relationship with Him. It all starts with our thoughts and what we choose to focus on. God knows our thoughts before we think them, and when we start to think His thoughts, we enter a unity that causes supernatural synchronicity. When we think about His ways, He begins to give a clear vision for our lives. In addition, He dispatches angels, His helpers who partner with us to do His will. Part of this process is called alignment—in which earth and heaven collide on our behalf.

REVIVAL CAME TO TOWN

This heavenly collision occurred when revival came to my hometown almost immediately after I asked a friend, "Where are these miracles Jesus speaks of in today's world?" I had never heard of revival and had no idea what I was walking into at the time. This particular revival happened in a tent and wasn't anything like any church I'd ever visited. It had a heavenly atmosphere in which the Holy Spirit moved, and I never wanted to leave.

As I look back now, I see the anointing God gave me to be His messenger as I led many to Christ even while still dabbling in sin. Clearly, something was still missing. I didn't understand why I was whole in spirit but so weak in the flesh. *Why can't I stop doing what I hate? Why can't I kick the old habits to the curb?* In church, I had heard the message, "Being saved doesn't mean you're perfect, but instead you're a sinner in need of Jesus." I settled for it because I didn't have the answer. I thought, perhaps I'm just made to love God while doing what is wrong in His sight, but it's okay because Jesus loves me regardless. I lived by this for years, but something felt off-kilter. It reminds me of the clear picture Paul painted of the battle between the flesh and the spirit and our need for deliverance:

For we know that the law is spiritual, but I am of the flesh, sold under sin. For I do not understand my own actions. For I do not do what I want, but I do the very thing I hate. Now, if I do what I do not want, I agree with the law, that it is good. So now it is no longer I who do it, but sin that dwells within me. For I know that nothing good dwells in me, that is, in my flesh. For I have the desire to do what is right, but not the ability to carry it out. For I do not do the good I want, but the evil I do not want is what I keep on doing. Now, if I do what I do not want, it is no longer I who do it, but sin that dwells within me (Romans 7:14–20 ESV).

The Bible tells us our bodies are the temple of God, also known as the house of God:

Or do you not know that your body is the temple of the Holy Spirit who is in you, whom you have from God, and you are not your own? For you were bought at a price; therefore glorify God in your body and in your spirit, which are God's (I Corinthians 6:19-20).

This means we need to be ready for some house cleaning. During the cleaning process, God will set the junk in our lives on fire until the rubble burns up into ashes. In return, He gives us *"beauty for ashes, the oil of joy for mourning, the garment of praise for the spirit of heaviness" (Isaiah 61:3 KJV)*. He does this by handwriting a testimony with our lives that becomes a living prophecy that testifies about Jesus.

The overwhelming call of God will continue to echo throughout your life in hopes that you will answer. You will hear the heavenly doorbell ringing as He waits for you to open the door. You may be like me and drown it out with the world's pleasures. You may ignore the call and say, "I'll answer it tomorrow." But it will never go away until you answer it.

Keep in mind, the devil counterfeits everything God does. Satan feeds his pride and ego by trying to one-up God in every way. Thus, he also calls you and tries to slip in undetected when you answer the call of God on your life. The devil does this by trying to enter the hidden cracks you've forgotten about. He is pushy, flamboyant, loud, and distracting, and he offers you a quick fix. It may taste good for a moment, but it will cause a form of spiritual cancer to enter your life later. It's like going through the drive-thru at a fast-food restaurant instead of waiting patiently for the meat at the steakhouse. What the devil offers is quick and cheap, but what God offers is nurturing and expensive. The blood of Jesus is costly, but He gave it freely on your behalf. Jesus paid your debt in full.

Answer the call today. Today is the day of salvation. Why wait? Tomorrow isn't promised to anyone. Stop blaming God for the chaos Satan has caused in your life. Jesus is calling, and you have no reason to wait. All you have to do is call out to Him, repent of your sins by confessing them with your mouth, and commit your life to Him. Go ahead and do it now.

But he was pierced for our transgressions; he was crushed for our iniquities; upon him was the chastisement that brought us peace, and with his wounds we are healed. All we like sheep have gone astray; we have turned—every one—to his own way; and the Lord has laid on him the iniquity of us all (Isaiah 53:5–6 ESV).

POEM: MY LORD

My praises are to you, my Lord,
Maker of heaven and earth.

The sun rises on your face.
The warmth fills my lungs.

Your breath gives me life.
My heart yearns for yours.

The clouds hold your tears.
The rains carry your spirit.

- Ruthie Dickey

2

THE REFINER'S FIRE

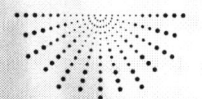

And I will put this third into the fire, and refine them as one refines silver, and test them as gold is tested. They will call upon my name, and I will answer them. I will say, "They are my people," and they will say, "The Lord is my God" (Zechariah 13:9 ESV).

So that the tested genuineness of your faith—more precious than gold that perishes though it is tested by fire—may be found to result in praise and glory and honor at the revelation of Jesus Christ (1 Peter 1:7 ESV).

For you, O God, have tested us; you have tried us as silver is tried. You brought us into the net; you laid a crushing burden on our backs; you let men ride over our heads; we went through fire and through water; yet you have brought us out to a place of abundance (Psalms 66:10–12 ESV).

Answering the call of God is just the first step on a lifelong journey. Once we've received Him, we enter the refiner's fire so our hearts can be purified. Oh, the fire of God hurts so good. It burns so deeply. This is the process each of the above verses addresses—the process of purification and refining—that each believer must go through.

Immediately when we get saved, the Lord starts the purification process. Yes, it's a process. Put on your seatbelt, and hold on for the ride, because shortcuts don't exist. It may take some time to get to the destination, but it's worth the wait. When we go through the fire with God, everything that isn't of Him will burn up, and all that remains will be of God. I call this burning-up process *spiritual heart surgery*. This is where we experience Jesus binding up our wounds (inner healing) and expelling demons (deliverance).

The Bible tells us that we are seated in heavenly places with Christ at the moment of our salvation. He has made the heavenly life available to us, but many Christians do not live it. So many of us know in our heads that we are "seated with Christ," but we haven't experienced the atmosphere of heavenly invasion that Paul described:

Even when we were dead in our trespasses, [he] made us alive together with Christ—by grace you have been saved—and raised us up with him and seated us with him in the heavenly places in Christ Jesus, so that in the coming ages he might show the immeasurable riches of his grace in kindness toward us in Christ Jesus. For by grace you have been saved through faith. And this is not your own doing; it is the gift of God (Ephesians 2:5–8 ESV).

When we experience the reality of this verse, everything changes. Consider this quick snapshot of my personal prophetic timeline. God called me while I was a child but I didn't answer that call until I was a teenager. Then, I was saved, but I still struggled with many strongholds. Soon after, I experienced inner healing and deliverance, which changed everything. Jesus had already blessed me with every spiritual blessing, but I had not grabbed hold of it. It was there, but I was unaware. The Bible says that people perish for lack of knowledge. I didn't know I could be purified—that I could experience Christ's inner healing and deliverance in order to enter into the spiritual blessings of life in Him.

When we hear others' stories, we then have the opportunity to make their ceiling our floor. In other words, what took one person a lifetime to understand can take you a few weeks. I encourage you to grab hold of what I'm saying and pull it into your life. The time is now. Be saturated in wisdom and understanding, which can only come by divine revelation of the Holy Spirit. Don't be moved or shaken. Don't turn to the right or the left but look straight ahead. Look and see what the Lord is saying.

I will never forget the day when a heavenly invasion swept into my room. I didn't feel anything special, yet I was in two places at once, and heaven was in my midst through faith. I was in the secret place of the Most High God. As my eyes opened, instead of seeing my bedroom, I looked beyond and saw an operating room in a hospital.

MY EXPERIENCE BEING TRANSLATED INTO THE HOSPITAL OF HEAVEN

I saw myself laying on the operating table in a hospital room and saw angels all around me. Jesus was my doctor, but we weren't talking. Instead, He took my heart out of my chest, and I knew He was doing supernatural heart surgery. He took my heart, which looked like a natural human heart, and washed it under water; I understood this was living water. I then saw words flowing into my heart from the atmosphere, such as love, peace, and hope. The kind smile on Jesus' face was enough, let alone getting personal heart surgery from the highest physician this world has ever known. I saw my heart transformed into gold within His hand, and then He put it into my chest, and I lit up. Once again, I saw Jesus' face. And standing behind Him, I saw my mother, Ruthie.

I pulled myself partially out of the vision and called my mom. I told her I had seen her in a vision, and we prayed that she would see it too. Suddenly, she could see herself looking at me in the operating room. She was standing behind Jesus, just as I saw her in the vision, and she saw the back of his head. A little girl came up to the hospital hallway's glass window.

I asked, "Mom, do you see that girl?"

She answered, "Yes, she has on a blue dress."

Incredibly, in my vision her dress was blue too. My mom and I were in the same vision and discussing it while sitting in our bedrooms over the phone, five hours away from each other on earth. Truly, the realm of the spirit has no limits.

The vision continued. I rose from the hospital bed, walked into the hallway, and saw my previous mentor, Joy. I saw her walk over to a lady in a wheelchair and lay hands on her while angels were standing behind her. The lady stood up, completely healed. A few days after I saw this, I called Joy and told her what I had seen in the vision. She said this meant something to her; in fact, she had written it out on her prophetic storyboard.

Later, my mom told me that, in the vision, when I walked out into the hallway, Jesus turned to her and held each side of her face. His face was like a bright shining light, and He blew on her, and the breath of God entered her, giving her more profound revelation. How incredible.

This operating room has become a place I've been able to take others to in the realm of the spirit. It's a place of the unseen, where we are seated with Jesus—a place of healing, hope, calling, and being chosen. I've discovered, in my time of waiting, that once you've experienced a vision, you can always go back to that place. However, I caution people to test everything they see in a dream or vision. No matter how intimate you are with the Lord, never allow yourself to enter a place of pride where you reject His teaching on testing the spirits:

Beloved, do not believe every spirit, but test the spirits to see whether they are from God, for many false prophets have gone out into the world. By this you know the Spirit of God: every spirit that confesses that Jesus Christ has come in the flesh is from God, and every spirit that does not confess Jesus is not from God. This is the spirit of the antichrist, which you heard was coming and now is in the world already (1 John 4:1–3 ESV).

BEING REFINED BY FIRE

Learning to step into supernatural encounters with God became an important part of my healing and deliverance process. When I truly answered God's call, I immediately entered into a waiting period of refining that some have called the wilderness. I had entered into a real relationship or encounter with a mysterious God who radiates love and is mighty to heal and deliver. The words in the Bible became living and breathing in the atmosphere of my life. When we begin to know the authority God has given us, we see the word of God come alive. Demons are cast out. The sick are healed. People are raised from the dead. The words in the Bible are alive because Jesus is alive. We were dead until we found Jesus.

"As you go, proclaim this message: 'The kingdom of heaven has come near.' Heal the sick, raise the dead, cleanse those who have leprosy, drive out demons. Freely you have received; freely give." (Matthew 10:7-8 NIV)

And in the book of Hebrews, the author tells us this about the word of God:

For the word of God is living and active, sharper than any two-edged sword, piercing to the division of soul and of spirit, of joints and of marrow, and discerning the thoughts and intentions of the heart. And no creature is hidden from his sight, but all are naked and exposed to the eyes of him to whom we must give account (Hebrews 4:12–13 ESV).

Truly, the reality of what God has made available to us is beyond comprehension. The more we experience, the more we desire. It's like following along a flowing river and admiring all the beauty. It becomes very enticing. We see the holiness and purity not found in the world. As I continued along this river of His presence, I wanted to find out more. I wondered, *Where does it lead? What else is along the way? What is this path I've found?* I longed for *the more* of God. There is more; there always will be. The closer we get to the Lord, the more we realize how limited the human mind is. When it comes to comprehending the fullness of who God is, we could spend a lifetime searching out His ways.

As we journey along this river I call *the waiting*, we learn more about who we truly are in Christ. We enter into the realm of understanding. We find out what it means for Christ to be in us and for us to be in Him, which is a two-fold dimension outside of time. Paul talked about this in Colossians, saying: *"To them God chose to make known how great among the Gentiles are the riches of the glory of this mystery, which is Christ in you, the hope of glory" (Colossians 1:27 ESV)*. He also told us, *"Set your minds on things that are above, not on things that are on earth. For you have died, and your life is hidden with Christ in God" (Colossians 3:2–3 ESV)*.

The secret place is *our life hidden in Christ*. He is the door to the dinner table where we dine with God. We go into this place, just like Jesus did, to hear what the Father is saying and see what He's doing, and then we do likewise. In this place, we are safe and hidden. The more time we spend with God, through the door of Jesus, and in the word of God, we will begin to hear the Holy Counselor speak to us. The Holy Spirit will reveal the truth to us, and we will see clearly what needs to be removed from our lives so we can access *the more* of God. That is what the refiner's fire is all about. It's not just a one-time experience; we will be purified throughout our walk with God. If we yield and say *yes* to the call, we will enter into the fire as many times as needed.

The fire of God allows things to happen to teach us what's important. Sometimes the fire burns things away, things like careers or relationships with people. Sometimes the fire of God requires us to move to a new geographical location in order to forge our spirit into maturity. Learning to be flexible and adapt to God's will is also a part of the refiner's fire. We must trust God even when things fall apart. God allows situations, not because He likes to see us in pain or causes the trial, but because faith must be tested. Often the kingdom of darkness is manipulating situations, causing pain in our lives. Regardless, God permits it to train us, allowing us an opportunity for spiritual maturity.

Spiritual war rages all around us, and we're being called into the fight. Whether we like it or not, there is spiritual warfare, which pours over into our natural lives. We can either be overcomers or get overtaken, the choice is ours. Some Christians say things like, "The devil attacks Christians much more." Lots of people talk about spiritual warfare against Christians. Let me offer a different perspective. People who aren't Christians are miserable too. People suffer from anxiety, depression, nightmares, insomnia, sickness, rage, addiction, and so forth. Satan hates people, period. Christian or not, he hates us and wants to destroy our lives. He is out to get us, but as Christians, we have authority over him.

As Christians, we should enter a place where we are seated high above with Christ, a place where warfare is under our feet. Being Christian won't take away the troubles of this world, but we inherit the Spirit of Truth, who brings comfort and guidance. We go through the refiner's fire to learn how to conquer the devil. He has already lost the game, but we must enforce our authority and put on the armor of God. The problem is so many Christians don't wear their armor.

Finally, be strong in the Lord and in the strength of his might. Put on the whole armor of God, that you may be able to stand against the schemes of the devil. For we do not wrestle against flesh and blood, but against the rulers, against the authorities, against the cosmic powers over this present darkness, against the spiritual forces of evil in the heavenly places. Therefore take up the whole armor of God, that you may be able to withstand in the evil day, and having done all, to stand firm. Stand *therefore, having fastened on the belt of truth, and having put on the breastplate of righteousness, and, as shoes for your feet, having put on the readiness given by the gospel of peace. In all circumstances take up the shield of faith, with which you can extinguish all the flaming darts of the evil one; and take the helmet of salvation, and the sword of the Spirit, which is the word of God, praying at all times in the Spirit, with all prayer and supplication. To that end, keep alert with all perseverance, making supplication for all the saints (Ephesians 6:10–18 ESV).*

POEM: ALL IN ONE

Lord, I know You.
Lord, I trust You.
For my soul is gladdened by the thought of You.
You give me strength.
You have set me apart.
In you, I have joy.
Your pleasure is in my smile.
Every part of me, You love.
No weapon can form against me
for You are my shield.
You take measures to protect me.
I do not fear evil because I have You.
No sorrow can stay within me.
Your spirit has filled me to capacity.
Your Son shines bright within me.
His taste is like honey.
Holy and glory, all in one.

- Ruthie Dickey

3

UNSEARCHABLE THINGS YOU DO NOT KNOW

Call to Me and I will answer you, and tell you [and even show you] great and mighty things, [things which have been confined and hidden], which you do not know and understand and cannot distinguish (Jeremiah 33:3 AMP).

Life in Christ is not meant to be dry and stagnant. He has so much more for us than many of us realize. He wants to introduce us to His Spirit and teach us the "unsearchable things" of His word. In the waiting, we realize our lives will never be the same, because truths that defy human wisdom and logic are opened up before us. When we read the Bible, we see that God doesn't act according to human logical reasoning. I absolutely love that God does all kinds of completely off-the-wall and unimaginable things. He is all-powerful and wonderful, and nothing is impossible with Him.

If you're still reading the Bible through your intellect, I invite you to throw out everything you think you know and allow the Holy Spirit to teach you. That is precisely the phrase He told me many years ago. I was like, *"But God, I've been studying Your word for years and I believe I know a lot."* Boy, was I wrong. The closer I got to God, the smaller I became, and the multilayers and facets of who He truly is began to unfold. The same will be true for you.

We can't move into the unknown by trying to know everything. We need to stop trying to figure it out and let Him reveal it on His timetable. We can go to Bible college, get all the knowledge in the world, or even sit under the most outstanding scholars that have ever lived. But nothing compares to sitting in the secret place of the Most High and allowing Him to minister to our spirit and soul. Many people graduate Bible college today not believing in the supernatural ways of God. He's inviting us into something better. God is Spirit, and we also have a spirit. Therefore, it's time to get spiritual. As Jesus said:

But the hour is coming, and is now here, when the true worshipers will worship the Father in spirit and truth, for the Father is seeking such people to worship him. God is spirit, and those who worship him must worship in spirit and truth (John 4:23–24 ESV).

I've learned from the studies of Dr. Ron Charles, a bible historian and founder of the Cubit Foundation, that the history of the Bible is vastly important, but I also learned that everything God did throughout the history of the Bible had a spiritual component. In addition, I learned that more documentation exists about Jesus Christ than all the books of the world could even contain. And I realized that every encounter with Jesus is wrapped up in a beautiful, miraculous ribbon of the supernatural and unexplainable ways of God. Therefore, we need both the logos and the Rhema word of God. The *logos word of God* is the written word of God, and the *Rhema word of God* is the living word, the spoken word, the revelatory word in which God speaks directly to us, Spirit to spirit.

THE SEVEN SPIRITS OF THE LORD

When the Spirit of wisdom and revelation comes, He will exude a flowing river of burning fire. The river of fire burns up all lies in its path. This river of fire flows violently in a specific direction, bypassing the human mind and reaching through the heart to touch the spirit of people. In this way, the Spirit purges the lies we've been believing.

Be ready when He comes, because you'll need to choose to receive. This download may be accompanied by a feeling of warmth or tingling, or you may feel nothing at all. Whether you experience a physical manifestation or not, your spirit will feel it as the Holy Spirit burns up the lies that have taken root in you. When the Spirit of revelation comes, we must be so sensitive to His nature, careful not to quench the Holy Spirit. Be sure to stop and write down what He is saying.

The Spirit of wisdom and revelation not only burns up lies, but He also makes way for God's supernatural mind. Paul explained it this way:

But, as it is written, "What no eye has seen, nor ear heard, nor the heart of man imagined, what God has prepared for those who love him"— these things God has revealed to us through the Spirit. For the Spirit searches everything, even the depths of God. For who knows a person's thoughts except the spirit of that person, which is in him? So also no one comprehends the thoughts of God except the Spirit of God. Now we have received not the spirit of the world, but the Spirit who is from God, that we might understand the things freely given us by God. And we impart this in words not taught by human wisdom but taught by the Spirit, interpreting spiritual truths to those who are spiritual (1 Corinthians 2:9–13 ESV).

When we experience blockage, the Holy Spirit does heart surgery to remove the blockage, giving us the mind of Christ and producing a healthy Spirit-to-spirit (*the Holy Spirit joined to our spirit*) flow. If we spend enough time in God's presence, His seven Spirits will come upon us and guide our steps. The prophet Isaiah outlined the seven Spirits of God:

> *And the Spirit of the Lord shall rest upon him, the Spirit of wisdom and understanding, the Spirit of counsel and might, the Spirit of knowledge and the fear of the Lord. And his delight shall be in the fear of the Lord. He shall not judge by what his eyes see, or decide disputes by what his ears hear (Isaiah 11:2–3 ESV).*

When the Spirit of the Lord comes upon us, we will realize we are on holy ground. When the Spirit of wisdom and understanding comes, we will know the exact steps to take and distinguish why this narrow path is the right one. When the Spirit of counsel and might comes, we will know where to go and have the strength to get there. Finally, when the Spirit of knowledge and the fear of the Lord comes, we will know where we have been in the past and where we are going now as we step into the heavenly places with Jesus. When that happens, we will be in awe of who He truly is. The more we search Him out, the more we become in awe of His glory. As Proverbs 25:2–3 says:

> *God conceals the revelation of his word in the hiding place of his glory. But the honor of kings is revealed by how they thoroughly search out the deeper meaning of all that God says. The heart of a king is full of understanding, like the heavens are high and the ocean is deep (TPT).*

And 1 Peter 2:9 echoes the privilege we have of being invited to encounter God in His glory:

But you are God's chosen treasure—priests who are kings, a spiritual "nation" set apart as God's devoted ones. He called you out of darkness to experience his marvelous light, and now he claims you as his very own. He did this so that you would broadcast his glorious wonders throughout the world (1 Peter 2:9 TPT).

We can think of the seven spirits of the Lord as the seven expressions of God, for the seven spirits of the Lord represent the nature of who He is and how He manifested Himself in Jesus Christ. The Holy Spirit reveals these things to us, and gives us the mind of Christ to understand how God thinks. God reveals His mysteries to those who are after His heart, and in the waiting, we learn that our hearts can be wicked. Therefore, we must cry out for God to create a clean and pure heart in us (see Psalms 51:10). In the waiting, we learn how to align with the mind of Christ as the Holy Spirit reveals the heart of the Father. As we walk through the refiner's fire, the Lord cleanses us by His blood (see Malachi 3:2), producing the pruning that is needed to humble us. This awakens us to the fullness of His expressions, the seven spirits of the Lord. Jesus Christ was able to walk in great power, although He left His deity to the side and became a man, because the seven spirits of the Lord rested upon Him. The spirit of prophecy foretold the coming of Jesus—His birth, ministry, position as head of the church, death, resurrection, and deity as God. I want to unravel one passage of scripture found in the book Isaiah, which outlines the seven spirits of God:

Then a shoot will spring from the stem of Jesse, and a branch from his roots will bear fruit. The Spirit of the Lord will rest on Him, the spirit of wisdom and understanding, the spirit of counsel and strength, the spirit of knowledge and the fear of the Lord. And He will delight in the fear of the Lord, and He will not judge by what His eyes see, nor make a decision by what His ears hear; but with righteousness He will judge the poor, and decide with fairness for the afflicted of the earth; and He will strike the earth with the rod of His mouth, and with the breath of His lips He will slay the wicked (Isaiah 11:1–4 NASB1995).

Here we see the seven spirits of God listed in a particular order:

1. The Spirit of the LORD
2. The Spirit of wisdom
3. The Spirit of understanding
4. The Spirit of counsel
5. The Spirit of strength
6. The Spirit of knowledge
7. The Spirit of the fear of the LORD

The order here is important, just as the order of instructions in an instruction manual is important. The order of God is a byproduct of unity in the Spirit. Unity in the Spirit produces an outpouring of the glory of God, which is His presence. In the passage above, we see first the Spirit of the Lord. The others are God's manifestations or expressions. Since the seven spirits of the Lord rested upon Jesus, I believe the same should apply to us since we are in Him. To see things happen "on earth as it is in heaven," we must be kingdom minded and earthly available (see Matthew 6:10). When Jesus came to earth, people thought He was coming to overthrow their evil government, but He came to destroy spiritual wickedness and establish a spiritual kingdom on earth. He did this through the seven spirits of the Lord, which were needed to establish the will of the Father. God gave Jesus supernatural help, and He does the same for us, all we have to do is ask. Even when we don't ask, God already does so much for us behind the scenes. I believe when we get to heaven, He will show us how much He intervened here on earth on our behalf.

The Spirit of wisdom and the Spirit of understanding work together as partners to renew our minds. This happens as we read the word of God, which transforms how we think and act as sons and daughters of God. Wisdom is knowing what to do, and understanding is knowing why something is done a certain way. This can work naturally, but even more so supernaturally. God is Spirit; therefore, He is supernatural. The Bible is a spiritual book full of spiritual encounters that display the spiritual ways of God. Therefore, to understand, we must tap into the spiritual.

If we understand God's spiritual ways, we will have the wisdom to know what to do with what God has given to us. Thus, when God visited Solomon in a dream, asking him what he wanted, Solomon answered by saying he wanted an understanding heart. This request pleased God, and He granted it, along with the wisdom to manage the people under him.

"So give Your servant an understanding heart to judge Your people to discern between good and evil. For who is able to judge this great people of Yours?" It was pleasing in the sight of the Lord that Solomon had asked this thing. God said to him, "Because you have asked this thing and have not asked for yourself long life, nor have asked riches for yourself, nor have you asked for the life of your enemies, but have asked for yourself discernment to understand justice, behold, I have done according to your words. Behold, I have given you a wise and discerning heart, so that there has been no one like you before you, nor shall one like you arise after you" (1 Kings 3:9-12 NASB1995).

The spirits of wisdom and understanding produce discernment. Next is the Spirit of counsel and the Spirit of strength. The Spirit of counsel assists in guiding our lives. Those in the occult engage with spirit guides, which are demons who seek to destroy the destinies of those they encounter. However, everything the devil does is a counterfeit of the authentic ways of God. We have received the Spirit of counsel who guides us and ministers to our souls. The strength of the Lord isn't found within us, but is made perfect in our weakness. When we are broken before the Lord, He can exercise His strength in and through our lives. The Spirit of counsel and the

Spirit of might give us insight into what to do and the power to do it.

Last, we see the Spirit of knowledge and the Spirit of the fear of the Lord. When they combine, a flow of faith manifests. It's not about just knowing God, but about being known by God. The Spirit of knowledge produces a divine relationship between God and people, while the Spirit of the fear of the Lord sustains the relationship. When all seven spirits of the Lord are resting on us, we enter into transfiguration. The evidence of this in a person's life is the fruit of the Spirit. This is not our fruit, but His, and as we are transfigured into His image, the result is that we walk in the fruit of the Spirit naturally. We can't obtain this on our own; the Spirit of the Lord does it in us.

DIVINE ENCOUNTERS WITH HIM

When we read the Bible in its entirety, we see that God was after one thing, a relationship with us. That is why He sent His only begotten Son, Jesus Christ, to die on the cross for our sins so that we might be healed, saved, and delivered. We begin living in unity with God as we walk through the door of Jesus and sit in heavenly places with Him. If we could understand this concept now, we would realize how close we are in relation to God in our current day and time.

My life completely changed when I stepped into a season of encounters with God and His supernatural power. This included divine inner healing and deliverance, as I talked about in the last chapter. I also experienced God's holy fire, the refiner's fire, melting away every unclean and evil thing. These were important steps to enable me to enter the secret place where the unknown things were unveiled— a place where God speaks to us directly. But the biggest hindrance to entering the secret place was the religious spirit, the same hindering spirit the Sadducees and Pharisees had in Jesus' day. He took holy vengeance against that evil spirit during His life on earth, and we must not allow it room in our hearts.

So today I encourage you to examine your heart. Do you hear

from God? Does He tell you unknown things? I'm not talking about things outside of scripture, but the depths of things, where deep calls to deep, that are found in the scriptures. You need God to disclose these things to you; you cannot simply understand them with only your human understanding. The scripture says you are a priest and a king within the kingdom of God and an ambassador of the kingdom of God sent to this earth. To do this, you must become like Jesus Christ, only doing what you see your Father in heaven doing and only speaking what you hear your Father in heaven speaking. So, the question is, *Do you hear Him? Do you see Him? Are you finding unknown treasures within His word?* If you answered *no* to these questions, repeat the prayer below to cast out the religious spirit and watch the scales fall off your eyes. Then be prepared to enter a place you've never been through the door that is Jesus (see John 10:9). It is a spiritual place, the secret place, the holy of holies, where you are seated with Christ in the heavenly realm (see Ephesians 2:4–6).

Pray this prayer to cast out the religious spirit:

Dear Heavenly Father, I come today before your throne of grace with confidence and ask for the children's bread of deliverance. I believe that Jesus Christ is the Son of God and the only door to Father God. He died on the cross for my sins and rose again. I repent of all known and unknown sin, including [*name specific sins*]. By the act of my will, I choose to forgive all who harmed or wronged me in any way, and today I walk them up to your altar and leave them with Jesus. *[List all of the people you need to forgive and what you need to forgive them for.]* Lord, I ask for forgiveness for the times when I have been angry with You and for the times when I've blamed You for the work of the enemy in my life. Forgive me for not having faith and trusting that You were working all things for my good. I receive Your forgiveness. Today I take a stand against Satan and all of his workers. I bind all principalities, powers, rulers, and spiritual wickedness over my geographical region.

I renounce you, Satan, and all of your workers. I come out of agreement with you, Satan, and all of your workers. I break every legal right that I have given you to my life. I shut all doors that I have opened to you. I belong to Jesus Christ. I do not want your workers influencing my life or your demons living in my holy temple. Luke 10:19 says I have authority to trample serpents and scorpions and all power over the enemy because of the precious blood of Jesus Christ. I command every controlling power from the kingdom of darkness within my mind to be plucked out at its root, and I command you to loose the hold you have over my mind and body right now in the name of Jesus. I renounce the hindering spirit of the Sadducees and Pharisees, the religious spirit, the legalistic spirit, the critical spirit, the judgmental spirit, and I command you by the authority of Jesus Christ to leave me now in Jesus' name [*Repeat until the evil spirit leaves.*] Holy Spirit, I ask You to come and fill up every room in my temple —my mind, will, emotions, body, and spirit in Jesus' name, amen.

Now is the time to arise, oh mighty warrior of God. The Lord has called you into His glorious waiting. In this place you will discover what was once unsearchable, the things unknown to you. Throughout the waiting, He will orchestrate the turning of the pages in your book, the one written about you before you were born, before you even lived one day.

For you formed my inward parts; you knitted me together in my mother's womb. I praise you, for I am fearfully and wonderfully made. Wonderful are your works; my soul knows it very well. My frame was not hidden from you, when I was being made in secret, intricately woven in the depths of the earth. Your eyes saw my unformed substance; in your book were written, every one of them, the days that were formed for me, when as yet there was none of them. How precious to me are your thoughts, O

God! How vast is the sum of them! If I would count them, they are more than the sand. I awake, and I am still with you (Psalms 139:13–18 ESV).

He wrote out your days, but you must choose to align with heaven. All of heaven is waiting for you to align with His word, the scroll about your life. When you do, you will start to see things from His perspective and hear things from His perspective. You will begin to uncover the things God hid, which were hidden for you so that you would go on a treasure hunt with Him. This journey will usher you into a destiny so far beyond all imagination, a place you can't yet fathom, beyond your wildest imagination.

POEM: HE REIGNS

I seek the throne on high.
My Lord, my Lord reigns.
He hovers above the earth.

The glory clouds fall.
His kingdoms rise.
His righteous bow down.

Our God, Our God,
Do not forsake us.
Our hearts yearn for yours.
Help us rise above the darkness.
Your light shines through.
Let your light shine.

Forgive our sins.
We repent with weeping eyes.
Your mercy we seek.

- Ruthie Dickey

4
THE GREAT STRIPPING AWAY

As for me, I baptize you with water for repentance, but He who is coming after me is mightier than I, and I am not fit to remove His sandals; He will baptize you with the Holy Spirit and fire. His winnowing fork is in His hand, and He will thoroughly clear His threshing floor, and He will gather His wheat into the barn, but He will burn up the chaff with unquenchable fire (Matthew 3:11–12).

The search for *the more* of God often leads us into a season of pruning in the wilderness, in which God removes anything that's not of Him and teaches us to hear His voice over the lies of the enemy.

Jesus came to baptize us with the Holy Spirit and fire. The fire of God is a place of intimacy, pruning, character building, and unquenchable passion, almost like an addiction, but in a good way. Some say that too much of anything isn't healthy, but I'm here to tell you that's a lie. Too much of Jesus is everything. We lack nothing when we have all of Him. I was baptized with the Holy Spirit and fire when I was nineteen, and my passion for Jesus has never left me; it has only increased.

How can we experience increase through the Spirit of God? The increase comes as we stay in the fire, where our hearts burn for Him. The increase comes with a decrease of self. As we decrease self, our pride is dismantled, and we're better equipped to follow God. This is essential to persistently seeking Him through life's trials, tribulations, and heartaches. These seasons will build character and produce good fruit if we keep our hearts in the fire. The fire of God is a place of trust where we unite with Him in body, soul, and spirit. Our soul and spirit are not the same, but they do work together. Our soul is made up of our mind, will, and emotions. The question we each need to ask is, *Is my soul in charge of my life?* God wants our spirit, in communion with His Spirit, to lead the way.

DISCERNING THOUGHTS

As God begins the process of stripping things out of our lives, He often begins by dealing with our thought patterns. Sometimes our thoughts come from an outside source. Sometimes our thoughts can come directly from demons. They whisper the lies of Satan into our ears, and it can sound so convincing that we believe it's our thoughts. On the other hand, some thoughts we have come from God, or His angels, who are sent to minister truth to our spirits. The final source of our thoughts is our own human mind. Understanding these three sources and learning to distinguish between them is crucial to submitting our soul to God. Below, I've included examples of each to clarify the difference:

Examples of satanic thoughts:

1. That's impossible.
2. You can't achieve that.
3. You're not loved, and no one cares.
4. Your life is pointless.

5. You'll never get married.
6. You're ugly, dirty, and unclean.
7. Nothing can cleanse you of the past things that have happened.
8. You're no good.
9. Nothing will ever change.
10. You should kill yourself.

Examples of God's thoughts:

1. All things are possible (see Mark 9:23).
2. You are loved and cherished (see Romans 8:38).
3. You are chosen (see 1 Peter 2:9).
4. There is hope (see Colossians 1:27).
5. You're not alone (see Joshua 1:9).
6. I'm proud of you (see 2 Corinthians 7:4).
7. Focus on God (see Jeremiah 29:13).
8. Good things will come from this (see Romans 9:28).
9. Not everything is as it seems (see 2 Corinthians 4:18).
10. I'll give you rest when you're tired (see Matthew 11:28).

Examples of human thoughts:

1. I'm happy.
2. I'm hungry.
3. I'm tired.
4. I'm upset.
5. This is a good idea.
6. I want to go on vacation.
7. I need a break.
8. I want to get married.
9. I love my family.
10. I want to start a business.

This is just a short list distinguishing between demonic thoughts,

God's thoughts, and our thoughts, but it gives a general idea of the differences in topic and tone. If you desire to align your thoughts with God and His will, say this prayer:

Lord, I come to You in the name of Jesus. I come to Your throne of grace with boldness, and I ask You to open the eyes of my heart so that I might know the hope of Your calling that You have set for my life. I speak to my soul, and I command it to submit to my human spirit, and now I surrender my body, soul, and spirit to the Holy Spirit in the name of Jesus. Lord, I ask You to align my life with heaven and the book You have written about me, as it says in Psalms 139. Lord, I ask You to cleanse my heart, and I repent of all known sin [list all known sin in detail now]. By the authority of Jesus Christ, I command every demon that entered through sin to leave me now and go into the abyss. I command you to come out of every room in me, and I renounce you now. I cancel your legal rights and revoke every curse in Jesus' name. Leave me now and come out now. Holy Spirit, I ask You to fill me in every room of my life to Your fullest measure so that I may serve You and know You and, most of all, so that You may know me. In the name of Jesus Christ, I command the blood of Jesus against the kingdom of darkness, and I bind up all retaliation in Jesus' name. Amen.

I pray you will be set free in your mind and soul today and begin to recognize the lies you've believed and the lying voice of the enemy. I also pray you will begin hearing the voice of God speaking over you. In this way, you will find freedom, and you'll never be the same. Go ahead right now and thank the Lord for all He will accomplish in your life today. Dare to believe deeper and walk in greater faith as you gain new understanding.

Sometimes, we make things so complicated when it comes to

our relationship with God. It's simple. We must become single-minded instead of double-minded. We must let the word of God and His thoughts rule our lives, or we will give way to the flesh and even the demonic. As Kenneth E. Hagin said:

> Often, I ask them if they have ever acted as though the Word is so. People must act like the Scriptures are true. If they don't act like the Word is true, they are walking by what their senses are telling them and not by what the Bible says. That's what is throwing them off. They're missing the faith realm entirely, which is based on what the Word says, not on what they see or feel.[1]

PIONEERS OF THE PAST

We need faith, and we need to embrace the baptism of fire, the stripping away, so that we can experience *the more* of God. So many people who have gone before us walked faithfully and pioneered with God. If we want to run our race with excellence, we would be wise to look to their examples. People like Kenneth E. Hagin, Kathryn Kuhlman, Smith Wigglesworth, Aimee Semple McPherson, Derek Prince, and so many others. Many people look at past generals in the faith and only see glory, glitz, and glam. But consider what goes on behind the scenes and the raw grittiness it takes to enter the place where Jesus will use you and set you on high. The golden key is surrendering daily and walking with humility. It begins when we allow our will to be undone. God isn't looking for perfect vessels, He's looking for available ones, sold out ones, fiery ones. Here are a few quotes from several spiritual generals about the life of faith and surrender:

Kathryn Kuhlman: The Heavenly Father does not ask for golden vessels. He does not ask for silver vessels. God asks for yielded vessels.[2]

Smith Wigglesworth: Real faith built the ark, but real faith did not shut the door. God did that. He does what you cannot do.[3]

Aimee Semple McPherson: We are all making a crown for Jesus out of these daily lives of ours, either a crown of golden, divine love, studded with gems of sacrifice and adoration, or a thorny crown, filled with the cruel briars of unbelief, or selfishness, and sin.[4]

Derek Prince: Each believer has some unique aspect of God's wisdom to reveal to the world and he reveals it by his testimony.[5]

Each person has an opportunity to come up higher with Jesus. We determine how high we go through dedication and communion with God. Our lives are a living testimony, and as we go from glory to glory, we experience the unimaginable and glorious goodness of God. Remember, *"God works all things together for the good of those who love Him, who are called according to His purpose" (Romans 8:28).* That means nothing is wasted in the realm of His glory.

Coming up higher will cost us something; it will most likely cost us everything. It will cost us family, friends, reputation, and fleshly desires. Our fleshly desires need to be undone so that the Lord's will can be done. I see it as a stripping away of everything we don't need —although we think we need it until it's gone—until nothing is left but God and us. When all we have left is God, then we have all we need. We don't fully discover this, of course, until we allow Him to strip everything that isn't of Him away.

Some things can be good but are not necessarily from God. So we need to get rid of even what is good and go for what is of God. For example, it might be good to start a church, but if God is calling you to be a missionary, you need to run after that. So many Christians get burnt out because they are entering into good things that God never called them to do. In the great stripping away, we realize this truth; once we become naked before the Lord, He clothes us with a new mantle. If you want God's will for your life, go after God, not whatever you think is good.

GOING TO NEW PLACES GEOGRAPHICALLY AND SPIRITUALLY

I grew up in Amarillo, Texas, and I never imagined moving anywhere else. But one day my world flipped, and I entered a place I didn't want to be. I had married my high school best friend, Ryan Butler. Shortly afterward, someone ran into his leg at work with a forklift, which forced him into surgery and time off and eventually led him to search for a new job and better opportunities. The Lord blessed him with a new job about four hours away, which seemed like a curse instead of a blessing at the time. Four hours isn't that far, but for me, it seemed very far. I had lost everything in my life that was comfortable. I did not realize that was the *exact reason* the Lord moved me in the first place; I was too comfortable. He knew what I needed for my growth. The Lord will take us out of our comfort zone to bring us into the unknown where He is.

The Lord moved me because I had a mixture of God and the world in my life. God is coming back for a bride (His church) who is not living in mixture, but who is uncompromised and unstained by the world. We all have stains, and we all have scars, but the blood of Jesus wipes us as white as snow. Some people say our scars become testimonies, and they do. But what if our scars disappeared and we walked out of being sinners and into the priesthood, being saints? Much of the mixture in my life came through some of my friends who claimed to be Christians, but who were walking on the broad road that leads to destruction. I'm not saying these people were bad or that I was any better. But I already knew, "*You are who you hang out with."* I may have been the worst of all my friends. Regardless, I needed to find company that would pull me higher. To do that, I first needed to embrace the stripping away.

If you want to run with warriors, you can't walk with the wounded. You can love on the wounded; we've all been there. Furthermore, you can pray for and care for the wounded, but if you're going to run with God, you must be trained with the spiritual snipers. My training all began with the stripping away.

POEM: SCARS GO DEEP

My scars go deep.
My pain is at hand.
My soul thirsts for you.
Have mercy on me, dear Lord.

I repent, and my heart is laid bare.
Forgive me, dear Lord, for my shame has been exposed.

Guilt has followed me most of my days. Open my eyes so I can see.
Forgiveness is on your lips.
My heart leaps for joy
For you are a just and merciful God.

- Ruthie Dickey

5
INNER HEALING AND DELIVERANCE

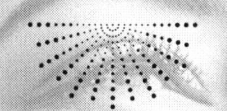

So often people receive salvation without realizing they also need inner healing and deliverance. We cannot step into our calling if we will not allow God to address the brokenness and bondage in our hearts. This was my experience for several years after I received Jesus. I was saved, but I still felt lost in many ways. We often don't know we're in darkness until somebody comes and turns on the light. Usually, that light gets turned on because of the prayers others are praying for us. I know the prayers of my mother, Ruthie, brought me into the kingdom and have pushed me forward in my walk with God ever since.

BEING CALLED AND BEING CHOSEN

The Bible tells us, in Matthew 22:14, that many are called, but few are chosen. It also says that God knew us before we were in our mothers' wombs. Recently, God told me, "You were anointed in your mothers' womb," and this brought me great joy, however I was even more ecstatic when God confirmed this word through my birth mom. Her and I connected on social media, and she told me that someone came to her in a dream, saying I was her golden child.

When she was pregnant with me, she would walk around repeating the phrase, "this is my golden child." Yet, growing up I felt abandoned and rejected, but God said I was chosen, and you are too, that's why the Holy Spirit got this book into your hands.

God knows everything; nothing is hidden from Him, not even people's thoughts. He has known who belongs to Him from the beginning of time. As a matter of fact, God knew this even before time existed. God is outside of time and space; therefore, He foreknew us before we knew ourselves. Paul talked about this in Romans 8:

For those whom He foreknew, He also predestined to become conformed to the image of His Son, so that He would be the firstborn among many brethren; and these whom He predestined, He also called; and these whom He called, He also justified; and these whom He justified, He also glorified. What then shall we say to these things? If God is for us, who is against us? He who did not spare His own Son, but delivered Him over for us all, how will He not also with Him freely give us all things? Who will bring a charge against God's elect? God is the one who justifies; who is the one who condemns? Christ Jesus is He who died, yes, rather who was raised, who is at the right hand of God, who also intercedes for us. Who will separate us from the love of Christ? Will tribulation, or distress, or persecution, or famine, or nakedness, or peril, or sword? Just as it is written, "For Your sake we are being put to death all day long; We were considered as sheep to be slaughtered." But in all these things we overwhelmingly conquer through Him who loved us. For I am convinced that neither death, nor life, nor angels, nor principalities, nor things present, nor things to come, nor powers, nor height, nor depth, nor any other created thing, will be able to separate us from the love of God, which is in Christ Jesus our Lord (Romans 8:29–39 NASB1995).

Being *called* means Jesus knocks at the door, and we answer it. But *being chosen* means we walk out our salvation with fear and trembling. By *fear and trembling*, I mean acknowledging the profound reverence of who God is and understanding that His will is perfect. It also means trusting in Him with our lives, even unto death. The word of God is medicine to our souls, and the word of God is refreshing, like rivers of living water flowing out of our innermost being (see John 7:38).

To access the fullness of this living water and to drink of the well that never runs dry, we must yield to the Holy Spirit and let Him undo everything that's been done in our lives. We must let Him undo all the religious garbage from our past, remove all the lies of atheism, dig up and dismantle the demons of the New Age movement, remove all false religion, and clean out anything else that was planted in our souls. We must let Him take away our unbelief and commission us into our assignments on earth. God doesn't care where we came from. He knows exactly where we came from; He saw us there, met us there, and pulled us out of there. Even now, God is pulling us out. He's pulling us out and pulling us into freedom. He is pulling us out of the prison chains of regret and shame. He's pulling us out of the pain and trauma of the past. He's pulling us out of the deep waters of suicide and depression, and He's holding our hands to comfort us. He is building trust so that we can know Him as Father.

SAYING YES TO GOD LEADING TO MY DELIVERANCE

God hears our prayers, and He wants us to hear Him. Prayer is meant to be two-way communication. He's not silent. He is speaking to us, but so often our "inner noise" drowns out His voice. So many voices speak, as we talked about in the last chapter, but the only one we should listen to is His holy whisper. Discovering and learning to walk in this reality has been an important part of my life journey. So many do not understand the cost of the oil (the anointing of the Spirit and the glory of God) needed to walk in the supernatural ways of God. Jesus paid for our salvation, but we find the oil poured out on our lives through relationship with God. We have to choose the oil.

God is everywhere, and God is always moving. God has never

left or forsaken us. We are never far away from God. In seasons when it feels like we are, we are just one step away. All we need to do is turn around and step into His arms. I had to figure this out for myself after my husband and I moved to a new town, made new friends, and started a new life. Unfortunately, that life wasn't centered on Christ. I had Christ on the side, and I loved Him, but I didn't know how to walk with Him. I was clueless about how to sit with Him or engage with Him. Mostly, I was unable to trust Him fully.

One day, an old friend called me and gave me a prophetic word that woke me from my slumber. Immediately, I felt chains breaking and hope seeping through the cracks of my heart, penetrating my soul and spirit. I had recently made a new group of friends, and perhaps they were suitable for that period of my life, but they were not a part of my future. Some people are only in our lives for a season. Because I had been abandoned as a child and had experienced so much trauma, letting go of anyone was hard. I had already let go of my old childhood friends, some of whom I had known most of my life, and now I could hear God's holy whisper telling me once again to let go and let Him come in.

That day, though it felt so hard, I decided to say *yes* to everything God was asking of me. Soon after, I walked through the doors of a random church and discovered, to my surprise, the atmosphere of heaven waiting for me in that service. Suddenly, my life changed forever as I met face-to-face with the deliverer, Christ Jesus. Before this day, I hadn't been delivered from the demons that had held me captive. Ironically, in a previous religious church, I had incorrectly learned that a Christian couldn't have a demon. Therefore, according to them, I was already delivered. Nonetheless, there I was, watching the darkness of hell release me in His holy name.

When I walked to the altar, the evangelist who was leading the service cast out a spirit of false religion. I remember repeating the prayer, not understanding what I was saying. Still, I meant it with my whole heart because I was desperate for freedom.

For three months afterward, I asked the Lord why a spirit of false religion had been cast out of me. I had never engaged in any false religions as far as I knew. I wasn't into the occult, witchcraft, horror movies, or anything of that nature. However, the Holy Spirit reveled to me, churches who quench the Holy Spirit and refuse his manifestations are in false religion, therefore this spirit entered me in what I thought was a Christian church. The spirit of false religion I had been delivered from was a strongman demon. That is why binding the strongman is so essential. Demons work in groups and have different rankings, so if we cast out the strongman, the minions under it will also leave. In my case, during deliverance from the strongman, the lesser demons of alcoholism and depression also left. I had suffered from depression all my life, and in an instant it was gone. For the first time, I encountered authentic joy, because when the Holy Spirit fills us, we have the all-consuming fruit of His Spirit. And His fruit tastes so good. Taste and see that the Lord is good (see Psalms 34:8).

I needed to be delivered from the spirit of false religion because so much of what I'd experienced of the Church did not represent God's heart. The web of false religion prevented me from understanding God's grace. All I'd tasted before deliverance was condemnation. The demons would put thoughts in my head, telling me I wasn't good enough, I wasn't going about it right, and I was alone. They kept trying to convince me that bad things would keep happening and I should just give up.

I had grown up in a religious setting, in a Methodist church, and then I went to a seeker-friendly church that was the extreme opposite after I got saved. In my opinion, neither taught authentic grace. This is why, until I experienced deliverance, I didn't understand God's grace. I always felt condemned. I believed I couldn't meet God's standards and I would always struggle with addictions. Of course, some of this had nothing to do with the church, but with my generational bloodline and the curses passed down through my DNA. However, the church didn't teach me the truth or help me get free of the lies. In the churches, I went to growing up, I was presented with two different personas of who Jesus was. One was a super religious Jesus while the other was a super cool Jesus who didn't really care about sin, because his grace covered it regardless. Neither of these represented the Jesus I know today.

Even if we're in Christian churches our entire lives, we can still be in false religion. This is why it's so vital to read the scriptures for ourselves and ask the Holy Spirit to teach us His word. This enables us to test everything we hear from a pulpit. The pastors the Lord had put in my life during those seasons were wonderful people, and I do not blame them for my experiences. We are all in the same boat seeking a relationship with God, and we all fail along the way. The key is to get out of the boat, look directly at Jesus, and walk on water. If we stumble, He will put out His hand and pull us out of the water just as He did for Peter.

Deliverance was a game-changer in my life. Deliverance truly gives us a chance at a new life. Many people from my past could attest to the transformation that happened in my life. It's nothing I could have done myself. Only God works miracles. He calls us to yield to Him, to sit with Him, to dine with Him, and to just be present with Him. When we do this, He leads us beside still waters and restores our souls. Throughout a period of three or so years, I continued to receive deliverance. Step by step, the Lord led me through progressive deliverance. Some of these deliverances happened because of divine connections; I was in the right place at the right time. God put several people in my path to mentor me and hold my hand all along the way. Although I love all these people, I don't see any of them regularly anymore. They came into my life for a season, at the right time and right place. One of these people, Annette Murray, deeply pierced my heart. She helped me grow in maturity as I began in my ministry work.

THE BIRTHING OF I WILL NOT KEEP SILENT MINISTRIES

That said, I founded a nonprofit ministry called I Will Not Keep Silent, founded on Isaiah 62:1: *"For Zion's sake I will not keep silent, and for Jerusalem's sake I will not be quiet, until her righteousness goes forth as brightness, and her salvation as a burning torch."* This ministry, which I started with my mom, is also the fruit of deliverance. We first experienced deliverance and then felt the call to minister deliverance to others.

The ministry was birthed when the creator of the universe joined together two fiery ones who desperately needed each other. Ruthie was a young woman who couldn't overcome the burning desire to have children, but her womb was closed. As time passed, she adopted two daughters, and I was one of them. Ruthie taught me about Jesus, and over time, I introduced Ruthie to God's relational and supernatural ways. Together we became a burning torch that hell could not quench.

However, a drastic turn of events swept through like a whirlwind, causing our light to dim. At this time, I had already moved to a different town for my husband's new job. In addition, Ruthie, who had suffered from Multiple Sclerosis and Rheumatoid Arthritis for more than twenty years, became deathly ill. The doctors said, *"She's near the end and has already outlived the days of these diseases."* I had been praying about my mother's healing for ten years and had extreme faith that she would be healed, but after receiving the bad news and seeing my mother bedridden, a dark cloud hovered over my mind. I was losing hope. Real hope—God's hope —always prevails. One day, as I listened to a song playing on the radio, I heard the words, "Don't you be afraid of the giants in your way, for you know that with God anything is possible." Once again, my faith arose.

Soon afterward, revival came to town, and Ruthie was completely healed and delivered from a spirit of infirmity. She's a walking sign and wonder. During that time, I also experienced deliverance (as I mentioned previously) and was supernaturally set free from many strongholds. Both of us were set free by Jesus and began operating in the gifts of the Holy Spirit. Furthermore, we were launched into ministry and on-the-job training with the Holy Spirit. In 2017, while I was lying in bed one night, I heard the Lord say to me, "You will have a ministry."

I asked, "What shall I call it, Lord?"

He answered, "I Will Not Keep Silent!"

I was reminded of a time in the past when a friend and I

contemplated starting a ministry with that name, but it didn't work out. After hearing the Lord mention the phrase, I Will Not Keep Silent (IWNKS), I called my mom and told her what the Lord said to me, and we remembered a prophecy she'd received in 2008 that said, *"You and Cher will work together."* At that moment, Christ set H*is* torch ablaze in our hearts.

Not very long after that, Ruthie and I were thrown into a spiritual battle with the enemy when a woman came to us needing deliverance. Although I, at the time, had little experience ministering deliverance, I felt the internal call as the Holy Spirit fell upon me, and we (through Jesus) administered deliverance to this woman. The captive was set free. Soon after, the word got out, and people came flooding to us for help.

After we spent time in the refiner's fire and the secret place, while also ministering inner healing and deliverance to those who came for help, I Will Not Keep Silent Ministries started to flourish. The I Will Not Keep Silent Ministries was birthed out of a series of miracles. Apparently, in the library of heaven, the days of the I Will Not Keep Silent were pre-written. When heaven aligns with earth, miracles become a reality. Our history as a ministry is His story (Jesus' story), and no one can shut doors the Lord opens.

I Will Not Keep Silent Ministries is a prophetic ministry equipped for inner healing, deliverance, dream interpretation, mentoring, discipleship training, and revivals through the power of the Holy Spirit. It's incredible how God infuses His glory into vessels of dust. If we go low in the secret place and step out of ourselves, we can enter through the door (Jesus). We will find pasture when we go in (ascend) and out (descend). In that place, we can see what the Father is doing and supernaturally pull things from heaven into the earthly realm. We say, "Father, let Your kingdom come and Your will be done on earth as it is in heaven!" The time is *now*!

THE STENCH OF BETRAYAL

The training process concerning ministry work wasn't easy, and it came with the stench of betrayal. Betrayal will come to all of us, and often it is part of God's divine plan to build us up in holiness. It's not as much about what people did to us, as it is about how we handle it. A friend once told me, "You never understand the value of loyalty until you experience the darkness of the deepest betrayals." Loyalty outshines all betrayal, and our loyalty is to God. To overcome betrayal, we must learn to walk in its antidote, loyalty to God and forgiving others. God showed us this in His relationship with Judas. I believe, "church hurts" are the hardest betrayals to overcome because we expect more from other believers. However, we must forgive and press forward and continue to gather with like-minded believers.

The grip of hell loosens as we hide in the shadow of the Most High and choose the road less traveled—the road of raw forgiveness. When we experience betrayal, if we do not forgive, the enemy has an open door for torment in our lives. Judas was always part of the plan in the life of Jesus, and He knew it. Judas shows us that betrayals will come, and when Jesus washed Judas' feet, He showed us His radical love. How we deal with people is a huge part of our inner healing process. Another part of refining is loving correction. God disciplines us out of love; those who won't receive correction are stupid (see Proverbs 3:12; 12:1). That said, when people do us wrong and inflict harm on us, we must understand that what they did was evil, but holding unto it keeps our souls trapped in regions of captivity. Often times we must also set boundaries, and in some cases we should stay away from that person. But true love doesn't return evil for evil, and the best revenge is no revenge, but handing them over to God to judge.

If we walk in communion, common union with Christ, we will realize that some people are for us and others are against us. Some who promise never to leave us will soon drift like the wind. Words of affirmation from those closest to us will become words of criticism and accusation filled with poisonous venom. The venom is usually a combination of ignorance, jealousy, and pride. The father behind this is the father of lies and the spirit of Leviathan.

DEFEATING LEVIATHAN

One of my most remarkable and eye-opening experiences with deliverance happened when I came face-to-face with Leviathan. At the time, I believed a certain situation was demonic (and it was), but the problem was that I had allowed pride to sneak in. I was determined to prove that I was right, and it almost got me into big trouble. Whether the other person was at fault or not wasn't important; this was spiritual warfare. As I wrestled with Leviathan working through this person, I had a revelation that stopped this spirit's assault against me.

I had spent hours defending myself and trying to prove my correctness, but then the Lord showed me the sneaky serpents' tactic behind the scenes. The Lord put a spotlight on my ugly pride, so I repented, turning from my sin. Then the Lord spoke to me very clearly, saying, "This spirit (operating through the other person) is trying to enter you, and it has a legal right if you open the door through pride. It's better to have peace than to prove who is right."

On that day, I began to learn that there is a time to speak and a time to be silent (see Ecclesiastes 3:7). When we are dealing with a spirit of pride (which works for Leviathan), it's not a time to speak. Arguing with demonic powers is pointless. I've undergone trial after trial with this until I finally passed the tests. Someone once told me, "You will continue to face the same situations until you learn what God is teaching you." My friend, you may fail the test repeatedly, but if you're walking with the Lord, you will eventually rise above the fray, just like an eagle in the sky.

Even though I had repented of my pride, my battle with Leviathan wasn't quite over. One night about a year later, as soon as my head hit the pillow, I felt like I'd been transported into a different place in the spirit. In a night vision, I saw a short, all-white, blacked-eyed demonic looking man visit me in a house that didn't look like my own. It all started when I saw a scorpion on the wall that transformed into a tarantula. Then my daughter came into the room and tried to kill the spider on the wall. In real life, my little daughter is an anointed warrior, so I wasn't surprised to see her trying to trample the enemy underfoot. What caught my attention was that the tarantula then transformed into a huge moth that picked up a backpack full of books. I thought to myself, *It is impossible for this moth to carry the weight of that backpack.* Suddenly, the moth transformed into a four-foot-tall demonic man (but he was not human) who was all white—deathly ill white in a very unnatural way. He had black eyes and no hair, and he looked very creepy and evil.

I asked, "How did you get here?"

He answered, "My master is Leviathan, and I was sent because of the prayers being prayed against you."

As I walked through this encounter, I felt the presence of the Holy Spirit guiding me every step of the way. I was not alone, and I did not have any fear, which was entirely supernatural. I was filled with the power and comfort of the Holy Spirit. The Holy Spirit then gave me a word of knowledge instructing me to ask the spirit what prayers were being prayed against me so that I could counteract them with the blood of Jesus.

I asked, "What are the prayers being spoken against me?"

The spirit seemed overjoyed that I had asked this and began to boastfully pray. While doing this, he was trying to touch me to impart these demonic prayers directly into me. However, I moved away as he moved toward me, and I prayed in tongues. While I did this, the demonic man had no power to touch me. He kept trying to say the prayers out loud and impart them to me, but he couldn't because of the power of the language of the Holy Spirit through tongues.

When he had finished boasting in his prayers, I said, "I am so glad that you just told me these prayers, and now I rebuke every word you just spoke and call them null and void by the power of the blood of Jesus." Now, these prayers appeared like Christian speech, but they were full of manipulation, which is witchcraft and pride. It's as if whoever was praying for me in the natural realm believed they were doing something good, yet they were praying out of their own will and seeking to accomplish their ways. It's like they were praying that God would take revenge against me out of their anger, and in return, they invoked demons. This demon was on a mission from Leviathan to wreak havoc on my life.

Thankfully, I had already humbled myself, distancing myself from this person a year before, and nothing could harm me. After I canceled this prayer with the blood of Jesus, the spirit lost all his power and fell into the wall, shriveling, and trembling. I asked, "What are you?" He replied, "I am a being." I then asked, "What type of being are you?" He answered by naming a specific classification of a demon in a language I didn't understand. This confirmed he was a demonic spiritual being working under the principality named Leviathan.

The next day, when I asked one of my prayer partners to pray about this encounter, through a word of knowledge my prayer partner saw a picture of someone's face in her mind—the person I'd had a conflict with a year before. Later that day, all of a sudden, that same person sent me a text asking me how I was doing. This confirmed my sense that the night vision and demonic encounter had to do with this person and possibly their prayers. We must be careful how we pray because some prayers cause warfare.

This experience helped me realize that the only way to combat a spiritual enemy is to be filled with the Holy Spirit and obey His every word. May this be a lesson to us all to be very careful how we pray. We should never pray from a place of revenge, pride, or manipulation, because those prayers invoke demons, not God. If we strive to walk in the light of Christ, we'll have to take some detours in the trenches of darkness, and we will learn the discipline and correction of the Father in heaven.

In the waiting it's important to receive necessary inner healing and deliverance so you can walk in purity and have a sound mind. To take it a step further, it's important to study the deliverance ministry of Jesus so you can learn from Him and understand your authority in Him. It's sad that in many bible colleges this subject is left out. We are living in dark times and as a believer you will encounter dark forces, so take this as a call to get equipped.

POEM: JOURNEY

My time is at hand.
My journey has been long.
My tears have become rivers.
My brow tastes the sweat within.

My well is overflowing with your love.
Thank You, dear Lord,
for the flood You have given me.
My sights are on high.
New depths have been made clear.

Reign in Your kings.
Reign in Your prophets.
Hear the calling, sons and daughters.
The time is at hand.
The trumpet has sounded.

The voice of the Lord has been heard.
Unity is the key.

One voice in unity.
The sound is now.

- Ruthie Dickey

6

DEEPER STILL

All great men and women of God go through long periods of waiting in which God shapes and matures them into His image. Sometimes the waiting is a timeline of processes in order to master a particular skill or a wilderness designed to build faith. Other times it's like the depths of the ocean, and we must dive into the unknown. Usually, when we think we have it all figured out, God whispers, "Deeper still."

GOING DEEPER THROUGH A DREAM

Years ago, I had a dream that illuminates this process. In the dream, I was at a church retreat, which meant I was in training, yet also receiving rest. I saw a medium-size boat at the dock and felt drawn to go over and check it out. Along the way, a snake came through the sand and tried to bite my ankle. I knew this snake represented lies from my past, which God was exposing so that I could leave them behind and press forward. After I defeated the snake, I walked up to the boat and met the captain, who represented the Holy Spirit in my dream. I sat with the captain in the driver's seat, and my husband sat behind me. We were in this together. We went out into deep waters, and suddenly the boat lifted high into the air and turned downward into a dive position. I realized we were about to go under and dive rapidly. It was as if the boat was a submarine. The captain whispered into my ear the name of someone I needed to forgive. He walked me through inner healing so that I could go deeper. As we entered the water, I felt scared, and he whispered in my ear, "Don't be anxious, for I am with you."

THE WILDERNESS EXPERIENCE

As we go deeper with the Lord, we are never alone. At times, we do enter a spiritual wilderness where we can't hear God speaking as we once did, but we still are not alone. Sometimes a lack of hearing God can indicate a need to forgive someone or to repent of some kind of disobedience. At other times, it's not that at all. The wilderness is like a faith-building training center where we come face-to-face with Satan and exercise our authority. It's a place where all we need is the written word of God. In the wilderness, fasting is required, and we learn to overcome temptation. It's a place of angelic activity as ministering spirits are sent to speak encouragement into our ears. And when we leave the wilderness, we walk out full of the Holy Spirit and power.

This is exactly what happened to Jesus (see Luke 4:1–14). The Holy Spirit led Jesus directly into the wilderness. *"And Jesus, full of the Holy Spirit, returned from the Jordan and was led by the Spirit in the wilderness for forty days, being tempted by the devil" (Luke 4:1 ESV).* And when He left, He was *full of the Holy Spirit and power.* It's interesting because we often go through wilderness seasons thinking something strange is happening to us, but the Holy Spirit leads us there to be strengthened and equipped for every good work. Without the wilderness journey, our destiny cannot be fulfilled. That is why we must praise the Lord in the hallway before the door even opens.

Jesus fasted while in the wilderness because when we fast by abstaining from food, our flesh gets weak, but our spirits are awakened, strengthened, and ready for action. When we're in the wilderness, we need our flesh to weaken. In this process, our spirits are made strong so that we can bypass the temptations of Satan. When our spirits are strong, our focus is not on the things of this world but on the unseen heavenly realm.

The devil's temptation can come in many forms, so don't be deceived. Sometimes it comes through friends that the Lord tells you to step away from, otherwise known as unholy alliances. It can come from ungodly entertainment and music and from the glamour of this world offering false hope through riches and fame. This is especially true here in America, where we're offered the lie of the "American dream," which invites us to sacrifice our souls to gain the world. But a life without Christ leads to death, and without Him nothing in the world can save us. If the lifestyle of the average American were some glorious dream, then we wouldn't see so many people needing medication, suffering from depression, using drugs, living in broken homes, and so forth.

We must not be tempted by life's luxuries to give up heaven's riches. We build our treasures in heaven, and the wilderness seasons prepare us for that. It's a place where we must decide—will we walk in faith, or will our feelings defeat us? What we feel is not always the truth. The facts aren't always the truth. For example, a person may be diagnosed with cancer, and the doctors say she will die. The cancer diagnosis is a fact, but the truth is God is a healer. The truth is found in God's word, and we experience His power when we believe His word as truth. The wilderness is a place where we learn to walk according to the truth of God's word.

In the wilderness, the devil knew Jesus was physically hungry, so he tempted Him where he thought Jesus was the weakest. But Jesus knew the word of God was all He needed. Through the process of fasting, He was strengthened spiritually and answered the devil, *"You shall not live by bread alone, but by every word that comes from the mouth of God"* (Matthew 4:4 ESV).

The devil will come to tempt us where we're weak, but the word of God is always the answer in those moments. We must find out what the word says to do about our situation and stand steadfast while doing it. It may seem like forty days or forty years, but the agony will slip away when we pass into the promised land. It's similar to a woman in childbirth. She experiences labor pains, but after the birth, the joy of holding her child takes all the pain away. We experience labor pains in the wilderness because we're birthing something of God to bring into the promised land with us. Even in the promised land, we will face giants. We will need whatever we're birthing to occupy the land.

When we walk in obedience, the favor of Almighty God rests on our lives. Sometimes, when we're walking under the shadow of God, the blessings of His favor chase us down. At other times, it feels as if we have to battle and fight through brick walls to take one step forward. When this happens, we must not be dismayed; this is not as worrisome as we might think. We have been chosen to battle against the brick walls and tear them down. This is the wilderness, and in it, God calls us deeper into Him. The fullness of joy comes when the battle in the wilderness is won.

THE POSITIONAL AND RELATIONAL ASPECTS GOD

In our relationship with Christ, two ends meet in the middle—the positional end and the relational end. Positionally, Christ has already done everything. The victory is already won, and the devil is defeated. The blessings are ours; the answers are yes and amen; salvation is available, healing is complete, and the curses are broken. Therefore, we have all we need. However, in life we face many hard battles where our victory seems to be blocked. When this happens it's wise to focus on the relational end of our walk with Christ, because positionally He's already accomplished everything. Relationally, we need to lay hold of what's already been done and learn to manifest it through deep intimacy, faith, and trust in God.

Positionally, we have the keys to the kingdom of heaven and are seated with Christ. Relationally, we must allow the Holy Spirit to reveal the hinderances in our lives that are keeping us from God's perfect will. Let's look at the topic of healing, since so many suffer with illnesses.

Healing is God's will. Jesus demonstrated this when He walked the earth. To receive healing, we must have faith, but many do have faith and haven't yet received healing. This can be difficult to understand. Sometimes these people have hindrances like a lack of knowledge of the truth of the word, sinful living, unforgiveness, a spirit of infirmity in the body (which requires casting it out), and so forth. The point is: positionally, healing is available to all who believe in the name of Jesus; however, the relational end requires us to enter into deeper intimacy with God, and when we've done all we can do, we hear the Lord whispering to us, "Deeper still." Once we understand our relational responsibility, we will see the branches of our life begin to blossom.

Jesus is the vine, and we are the branches, and if we remain in Him, we will bear fruit. As Jesus said, *"I am the vine; you are the branches. Whoever abides in me and I in him, he it is that bears much fruit, for apart from me, you can do nothing" (John 15:5 ESV).* The hidden clue in this verse is "remain *in* Him." There is a secret place in Christ, like a room or a house we sit inside. Jesus provides a place within Himself. He's the door to the secret place where we are to commune with God directly. He's in us, working through us, and we are in Him. It's two-fold. Positionally, Jesus is at the Father's right hand in heaven, and we are seated right there with Him in heavenly places. Relationally, Jesus is in us, and we are in Him. Relationally, Jesus is working through us because of the finished work of His shed blood by the power of the Holy Spirit. We are clothed in Christ. Paul wrote, *"For you are all sons of God through faith in Christ Jesus. For all of you who were baptized into Christ have clothed yourselves with Christ" (Galatians 3:26–27 NASB1995).* That is how close we are to Him. We wear Christ as we wear our clothes.

Several years ago, the Lord gave me a vision to teach me about His wonderful grace. While sitting in my living room talking to Jesus, I fell into a vision and saw a bright, blinding light. Jesus walked over to me, where I sat on the couch, and He sat down directly into me. He and I were one. His light shone through and around me as if He was my clothing. Then the Holy Spirit said, "You are clothed with Christ". That day, that verse became alive to me.

DEEP CALLS TO DEEP

When deep calls to deep, the word of God becomes a waterfall flowing over our lives. The waves carry us to a new place, and we find ourselves in the prayer chamber. The psalmist described it this way:

> *Deep calls to deep at the sound of Your waterfalls; all Your breakers and Your waves have rolled over me. The Lord will command His lovingkindness in the daytime; and His song will be with me in the night, a prayer to the God of my life (Psalms 42:7–8 NASB1995).*

Prayer is where we meet with God and practice living in His presence. God is ever-present with us at all times, even more so during the hard times. Practicing His presence is something we master in the waiting with God. The presence of God changes everything. That's why, when the disciples were beaten, thrown in prison, and faced tremendous persecution, they were still full of joy. His presence was always with them, and they learned how to practice being in His presence through prayer.

Yet so many people don't understand prayer. They view it as a religious act with memorized, rehearsed words. For many, prayer is just an act, a list of items to check off, or a duty to get done. None of this sums up the essence of prayer. In church or ministry settings, people commonly treat prayer requests like a grocery list. They have so many requests that people pray quick, check them off, and move to the next. It becomes overwhelming and a chore. That isn't prayer. Prayer is an invitation to go deeper in God.

In its simplest form, prayer is two-way communication between God and us. Prayer happens when we talk to God and He answers. Jeremiah 33:3 says, *"Call to me...,"*—that's our prayer. Then it says, *"...I will answer you..."*—that's God's response. Finally, it says, *".....and I will show you great and mighty things you do not know."* In prayer, God shows us things we don't know but that have the power to change our lives, the atmosphere around us, and those we influence. In the place of two-way communicative prayer, God wants to speak to us even more than we want to listen.

For this reason, it's vitally important to keep a journal and write down all that He says, as well as looking it up in the Bible to confirm that we're hearing God. What God says to us will never contradict the Bible. When God speaks to us directly, this is called the *Rhema* word (revelatory word) of God. However, the *Rhema* word of God will always come full circle with the *Logos* word (the Bible). We must test what we hear. After teaching on the prophetic for many years, I have heard some students say the Holy Spirit is telling them some very crazy stuff that doesn't line up with scripture. When I hear that, I know it's not from God. Be careful not to fall into this trap; one of the devil's primary tools is deception.

HOW TO PRAY EFFECTIVELY

Sometimes very well-meaning people say there is no wrong way to pray, but I want to challenge that statement by saying there is an *effective* way to pray. I want my prayers to be effective; I want my prayers answered. To see our prayers answered, we need to spend purposeful alone time with God. We need to make Him our priority, read the word of God, and speak out loud the revelation He gives us. His word is as a solid rock, unwavering. We can stand on it. We do this by decreeing and declaring the word of the Lord over our lives.

Let's look at the word *decree* by definition:

Decree
noun; a formal and authoritative order, especially one having the force of law:
A presidential decree.
Law. a judicial decision or order.
Theology. is one of the eternal purposes of God, by which events are foreordained.
verb (used with or without object), de ·creed, de ·cree ·ing.

To command, ordain, or decide by decree.[1]

Decreeing God's word is more powerful than we even realize. When we stand and pray according to the scripture—which means we speak forth a Bible verse out loud over a situation—we are activating God's voice in our situation. We're enabling God's breath to blow, which is like a powerful wind that changes negative circumstances. When we declare the word of God, we're simply coming into spiritual agreement with it, which activates the angels to work on our behalf. Angels don't answer our demands, but they do hearken to the word of God. As Psalms 103:20 says, *"Bless the Lord, you His angels, mighty in strength, who perform His word, obeying the voice of His word" (NASB1995)*. This type of prayer aligns us with heaven.

When we pray this way, we're changing the atmosphere all around us. This happens whenever we speak the word of God out loud. All things in heaven and on earth were created by His voice, the everlasting breath, the decree of God's mouth. Whenever we speak the word of God, His word will not return void. It stands forever and has supreme authority; everything else must bow down to God's word. The word of God will accomplish what He sent it to do. As my favorite Bible verse declares:

So will My word be which goes forth from My mouth; it will not return to Me empty, without accomplishing what I desire, and without succeeding in the matter for which I sent it (Isaiah 55:11 NASB1995).

Dynamite power resides in the word of God. Yes, at times we have to wait for His word, and this takes faith. We must be sure of what we hope for and certain of what we cannot see. We must simply believe. It will come to pass because God is a just judge, and His word is like a hammer. The word of God never fails.

In order to understand the true definition of prayer, we must break out of the rut of religious works. When we talk to God, we enter a common union with Him. We answer His call to go deeper still, and this is often done through prayer. It's a place where we humbly come to Him, unloading all of our cares because He truly does care for us. We also repent of the sin that clings so close, and we listen to His soft still voice that brings forth wisdom and revelation as loud as thunder. If we don't unload all the baggage, it will boggle our minds. We must first deal with the mess inside of us, and often, God will lead us into inner healing and deliverance. Prayer is like a spiritual garden. We will begin to see green grass where there were only weeds before. By the power of the Holy Spirit, fresh seed will be planted, and as we read God's word, the seed is watered. The sun (the Son) will shine and cause the seed to grow.

Prayer is every day, all day. When we pray, we are talking to the Holy Spirit who then reveals the heart of the Father (see 1 Corinthians 2:10-13). We get to talk to Him as we talk to a friend, but unlike our friends, the Holy Spirit is always with us. We are never alone. He is ever-present in our lives. We should speak to Him often and allow Him to unveil the mysteries of heaven that are waiting to invade every circumstance of our lives. When we hang out with the Holy Spirit, we will enjoy His company because we will see signs, wonders, and miracles flowing forth from a well that never runs dry.

Jesus said, In Matthew 16:19, that He has given us the keys of the kingdom of heaven (see Luke 17:20-21). The word *keys* is plural, meaning more than one. It's like a spiritual keychain of keys that God gives us to open spiritual doors, gates, and portals. I believe one of these keys is prayer. We open the door that is Jesus through our prayers and enter into the throne room of God.

DIFFERENT TYPES OF PRAYER

To become effective in praying, we must understand the different types of prayer. One of the most important is intercessory and interceptor prayer. When I say interceptor, I'm referring to being like a watchman, seeing the schemes of the enemy from far off, and annihilating them before the plans come forth. In intercessory prayer, a person intercedes on behalf of someone else. This is the type of prayer described in Ephesians 6:17–18:

> *And take the helmet of salvation, and the sword of the Spirit, which is the word of God; praying always with all prayer and supplication in the Spirit, being watchful to this end with all perseverance and supplication for all the saints (NKJV).*

Jesus also does this for us (see Romans 8:34). In church groups, we often take prayer requests and compile a list of people to pray for, which can become quite a task. It shouldn't be this way. Instead, I believe God will lay people on each intercessor's heart to pray for. The rest He will assign to other intercessors. When we invite the Holy Spirit to invade the prayer requests, He will tell His intercessors what's on the Father's heart for each person, and all the prayers will be targeted and purposeful. In corporate intercessory prayer meetings, the most important thing is unity. Not everyone agrees on everything, but if we find the points of unity and align those with scripture, we will see the flow of the Lord enter those prayer times. In the flow of the Spirit, we will be carried away into other dimensions of prayer that we never thought possible. Prayer is not boring. If prayer to you is mundane and boring, then you're not experiencing prayer. Prayer is not religious; it's two-way relational communication, speaking and listening. It's the way we go deeper in God, and there's nothing boring about that.

Another form of prayer is warfare prayer. This kind of prayer is what I know best and where I gained my spiritual muscles for this season. The waiting season is full of warfare. Positionally, Christ defeated the enemy on the cross and became the curse so that we are released of every curse (see Galatians 3:13). However, relationally, we take the keys to the kingdom and put them into action. Many people are waiting for God to do what He already did and fail to realize that part of the waiting is that God is waiting on us. We must put on the full armor of God to withstand the enemy; this isn't automatic. We must receive the salvation that's available. It's a choice, just like it's a choice to brush off the generational or self-imposed curses on our lives. The word of God is all we need in order to see freedom—but we have to choose that step.

Scripture says we are new creations. The old is gone (see 2 Corinthians 5:17). This is true spiritually, but mentally and physically, many Christians still live in bondage. Our spirit beings are made new upon salvation, but the rest requires us to enter a relationship with Christ. God warns us to watch out for Satan, who is like a lion looking for someone to devour (see 1 Peter 5:8), and He tells us not to give a place to the devil or we will become shipwrecked (see Ephesians 4:27). He says this because, if we aren't diligent, the enemy will come in us to steal, kill, and destroy the will of God for our lives. Taking a stand against Satan and his workers requires warfare prayer in which we extinguish the enemy's fiery darts.

When we do inner healing and deliverance sessions, we allow the Holy Spirit to reveal everything hidden and make it known. When the Holy Spirit does the inner healing (healing of inner wounds) and deliverance (casting out of demons), it's much quicker and more effective. That is what authentic warfare looks like. He truly does fight our battles. He just needs a yielded soldier ready for service. It's time to get our boots on. In these last days, I'm convinced that if the bride of Christ was a picture, we'd see a woman in a wedding dress and army boots.

At times, when God releases His prophetic destiny over our lives, right afterward all hell breaks loose. Hell is after our destiny and working hard to destroy the breakthrough that's about to burst forth. For this reason, warfare prayer includes waging war with the prophetic words over our lives. The apostle Paul urged Timothy to wage war with the prophesies given to him, and we should do the same.

This charge I commit to you, son Timothy, according to the prophecies previously made concerning you, that by them you may wage the good warfare, having faith and a good conscience, which some having rejected, concerning the faith have suffered shipwreck, of whom are Hymenaeus and Alexander, whom I delivered to Satan that they may learn not to blaspheme (I Timothy 1:18-20 NKJV).

In the waiting season of my life, I waged war with almost every prophetic word I'd received. It didn't come easy in this past season, but it had a divine purpose. I was in spiritual boot camp and learned how to war over my life just as armies war against evil governments trying to occupy their land. I'm going to the land filled with milk and honey. I know giants live even in the promised land, and I will run after them headfirst. That's why God gave us armor for our front side; He has equipped His courageous bride to face threats directly. We will not always have to wage war for the prophetic destiny of our lives, but for a season, we must war and contend. It is all in the waiting.

A third type of prayer is travailing prayer in the spirit, which is often done without words. Sometimes these prayers are released in tears, but thankfully, God collects our tears in a bowl. If we don't give up, those tears will be used to water us in the coming seasons, just like the rain that falls in a drought. We must never forsake praying in spirit and truth which incorporates travail prayer. One of the best ways to do this is to let the Spirit of truth pray for us through praying in tongues (see Acts 2:4). The Holy Spirit prays but uses our mouths and utters mysteries on our behalf (see 1 Corinthians 14:2; Romans 8:26). Praying in tongues leads to fruitfulness as God's will is done in our lives.

If you haven't received the gift of tongues, repeat this prayer and believe you will. You will start out with non-identifiable baby talk, just as when you were a child and learned your ABCs in syllables. You're on the right track if you don't understand what you're saying. Tongues is a place of prayer, belief, and faith, not logic and reasoning. After all, God loves to work in supernatural and mysterious ways. Praying in tongues is a part of this. The Bible talks about various types of tongues, but here I'm only covering the type of tongues that builds up your inner being. Pray this prayer to receive tongues:

Lord Jesus, I come before Your throne of grace humbly yet boldly asking for Your will to be done in my life. Your word says if I ask You anything, according to the word, it will be mine. You say that You desire for all people to speak in tongues (see 1 Corinthians 14:5), so I ask Holy Spirit to come into me, fill me up, and speak through me. I receive the gift of tongues now by faith.

CAUTIONS ABOUT PRAYER

Now that we've talked about several important types of prayer, let's talk about what prayer is not. Sometimes, if we look at what something is on a micro level, we can avoid what it is not on a macro level. If we do prayer effectively on a smaller level, it will blossom on a larger scale. If we do it wrong, we can get into deep darkness just as quickly. Most importantly, prayer is not getting our way. I learned this the hard way. Simply asking God for something isn't deep prayer; deep prayer happens when we also listen to God and confirm our prayer requests in His word.

I have prayed for certain things and later felt thankful my prayer requests didn't happen. Sometimes we don't see the bigger picture, and we can end up praying presumptuously. As we enter into authentic prayer, we build trust in the Lord and discover that what we may have perceived as unanswered prayer was the answer we needed all along. God's communication isn't limited to our understanding. Communicative prayer sometimes ends in a mystery, and the answer comes within the realm of eternity. I believe some prayers are answered when we pass fully from this life into death, which is actually the fullness of real life. Death on earth is life to those in Christ. That's why when we pray for someone to live, but that person dies, we shouldn't get angry with God. Instead, we need to understand that some prayers are answered after this life. He will explain and we will understand later. What matters is that we must trust in the Lord regardless of whether we get our way.

We must also be cautious not to cross spiritual prayer borders. Prayer has borders and boundaries, just like the world's nations, to protect us from an enemy invasion. Practically speaking, this means we never want to cross the line into prayers of the flesh that produce witchcraft. In chapter 5, I told the story of a time when a demon came to me because of witchcraft prayers prayed against me. We have all fallen into this trap. We have all prayed wrong prayers, and we must repent and cancel any demonic assignments sent forth from our lips. In the simplest form, witchcraft prayers are when we seek to control others and ask God to move on our behalf. The only god that moves in response to those prayers is the god in this world, Satan, and his agents (see 2 Corinthians 4:4). Galatians 5:19–21 speaks about the works of the flesh, one of which is witchcraft.

If we pray out of pride, a vengeful heart, or control, we are praying in the flesh and working with witchcraft. Witchcraft isn't just conjured up by ladies in pointy hats with cauldrons; it can also work through believers who are under deception. The best way to safeguard ourselves from these demonic prayers is to always examine our hearts, humble ourselves, seek wise counsel, and bless those who curse us. If we feel we are being attacked by people who have demons or powers working behind them, bless the people but target the dark powers in prayer. We're not battling against the people, but the spiritual wickedness working in them, with them, and through them. As the apostle Paul wrote, *"For we wrestle not against flesh and blood, but against principalities, against powers, against the rulers of the darkness of this world, against spiritual wickedness in high places"* (*Ephesians 6:12 KJV*).

One of the best prayers to pray is Psalms 35. Praying scripture is powerful and effective. We must never stop praying and talking with God. Persistent and constant prayer is our lifeline. As Paul said:

Let love be genuine. Abhor what is evil; hold fast to what is good. Love one another with brotherly affection. Outdo one another in showing honor. Do not be slothful in zeal, be fervent in spirit, serve the Lord. Rejoice in hope, be patient in tribulation, be constant in prayer. Contribute to the needs of the saints and seek to show hospitality (Romans 12:9-13 ESV).

In the waiting, we need to contend in prayer; the lifestyle of prayer will take us deeper still.

POEM: OVERFLOW

Jesus, you are my joy and peace.
Like rivers of living water, You flood my soul.
Your presence gives me calm.
My life belongs to You.
I follow Your ways.
Your spirit sings of love,
Love without ceasing.

My heart overflows with the compassion You have for me.
I am not worthy, yet You call my name.
"Come hither," You call, and I am filled.

Joy unimaginable goes deep within my spirit.
I sing You praises of thanksgiving.
My heart leaps at the thought of You.
Your still small voice encourages me.
You lift me up when I am down.

No words can compare, no words can explain the worthiness of Your name.

Jesus, You are my everything.
Your blood is my protection.
I declare the blood of the lamb.
Who was and is and is to come.

- Ruthie Dickey

7
PROPHETIC PUZZLES

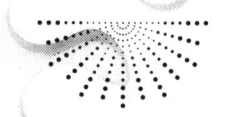

God gives us clues to our destiny—prophetic puzzle pieces. Throughout our lives, He drops hints leading us toward His calling for our lives. But we must learn to recognize those hints and begin putting the prophetic puzzle pieces together. This is an important part of the season of waiting we all walk through.

The concept of prophetic puzzles came to me through divine revelation from the Holy Spirit. He speaks a spiritual language we can understand through words, visions, and dreams. He speaks to us in a way that makes the Bible come alive. I never realized how much my life has intertwined with scripture until I received this revelation.

We all have our own individual prophetic puzzle that connects to an even bigger puzzle. Each person's whole life comes together as a puzzle creating a single piece on God's overall prophetic puzzle. Our lives are each valuable because we are a piece of something so much greater and vaster than our minds can even imagine.

From the time we were born until now, our life puzzles are being formed. The easiest way to put together a puzzle is to frame it with the edge pieces first. Therefore, we must look first for the outer parts of the puzzle. These include the day when we were each born and the milestones that have shaped our lives. After the frame is assembled, some missing pieces start to come into place, but the puzzle still looks funny and jagged. But even the unfinished, jagged parts will, in the end, come together for a beautiful masterpiece.

This happens as we align with God's will for our lives. If we choose not to align with His will, we will instead put together a picture of Satan's destiny for our lives and thereby forfeit God's plan. Satan comes to kill, steal, and destroy every step of the way (see John 10:10). However, God brings life to every dead part. He brings water to the dry land, restoration to the broken, and peace to the chaos. He makes all things beautiful in His time (see Ecclesiastes 3:11).

When we are running after God, our individual puzzle pieces will continue to connect. Many connections are interwoven through divine moments, divine friendships, and divine doors that are shut and opened at the divine times God has set. One of the most miraculous moments of our prophetic puzzles is when we were woven together in our mothers' wombs. If more women realized this, many of them wouldn't have aborted their babies. If you did have an abortion, God still offers hope. He has grafted your child into eternity with Him. Your child originally belonged to God, and He gifted the child to you, but now your child has returned to the author of love. Love covers a multitude of sins (see 1 Peter 4:8). Psalms 139:13 speaks of the way God wove us together and planned our lives before we were even born.

How incredible that God has ordained each of our days before even one of them happened. God had a plan for our lives before we were born, and He wrote it down. He knew all the days He had planned specifically for each one of us. That is why it's prophetic. The prophetic nature of God points to things in the past and foretells the future. God already knew our past and future before He created the earth's foundation. Knowing this, He chose us to be birthed during this time in human history because we have missions to fulfill. Now we just need to seek it out. And as we seek, He will mold us into His image.

"But now, O Lord, You are our Father, we are the clay, and You our potter; and all of us are the work of Your hand" (Isaiah 64:8 NASB1995).

God is outside of time and space, and so are our prophetic puzzles. We are living this life as spiritual beings in Christ who are engaging in the human experience. Our puzzles aren't just about the natural everyday life, but also (and even more) about our spiritual lives and the realm of the unseen. Because our lives are puzzles that then transform into puzzle pieces in God's great puzzle, our lives are interwoven with others in the body of Christ. Our lives cross the paths of others for a reason. Sometimes these crossings are good, and sometimes they're awful. Nonetheless, they shape our puzzles, allowing us to connect to the bigger puzzle that is outside of time and space in a dimension not seen by the natural eye.

Not one piece of the puzzle can be thrown away. That would create holes in God's puzzle. Thus, God takes all the bad things that have happened in our lives and turns them for good. He who started this puzzle will put it together correctly with divine precision. Just as Paul said:

"For I am confident of this very thing, that He who began a good work in you will perfect it until the day of Christ Jesus" (Philippians 1:6 NASB1995).

MY PERSONAL PROPHETIC PUZZLE

Now let's look at a few of my own puzzle pieces to demonstrate exactly how they come together. When I was in my mother's womb, she chose life. Therefore, knowingly or unknowingly, she aligned with heaven, and I'm so grateful for that. One side of the frame of my puzzle is my childhood, in which my sister and I were abandoned in a car with a young girl, who eventually called for help. This forever shaped my life. This unknown girl was a huge part of my puzzle. Even though I'll probably never meet her again, her puzzle connecting to mine became a prophetic piece of my life. After my season in foster care, Ruthie Dickey later adopted me, raised me, and taught me about Jesus—another puzzle piece. In 2008, Ruthie received the filling of the Holy Spirit and received a prophetic word stating we would be working together. We didn't know it then, but that prophecy would help frame the ministry sector of our lives. If we hadn't yielded to God's call, that puzzle piece would be incomplete and still missing. Sometimes this happens. We encounter parts of our lives that need to be completed. In those moments, we need to turn around and run back to the Father. Doing this will activate our puzzles again. The prodigal son's destiny was divinely interrupted and restored by one simple choice to turn around. The same will be true for us.

I spent most of my preteen and teen years running from God and living in rebellion. I know what it's like to be surrounded by demons, to face addiction, to be suicidal, to experience abuse, to be abusive to others, to feel shame and guilt, and to be full of pride. If I didn't have those darker pieces in my puzzle, I wouldn't have the radical love for Jesus that I have now. Those who have been delivered of much love Him much. These pieces connected to my inner healing and deliverance puzzle pieces, which birthed a ministry that is connected to many others and their individual puzzles.

GOD'S PROPHETIC PUZZLE

The Bible is God's prophetic puzzle—the Old and New Testaments coming together to produce the most extraordinary love story ever told. The apostle John wrote, *"For the testimony of Jesus is the spirit of prophecy" (Revelation 19:10).* The spirit of prophecy is the driving force that connects the dots of our scriptures. The fullness of the gospel of Jesus Christ is one big puzzle from Genesis to Revelations, and we all have a role to play. The Old Testament is a foreshadowing of the New Testament. The old covenant had to take place in order to produce the new covenant. Bible prophecy itself foretells all that was and all that is to come. As we live out these last days, we ought to pay attention to Bible prophecy. To grasp what's really going on, we should pay attention to the Hebraic calendar. God still moves off this calendar today and it intertwines with current events. In this book, I won't be covering all the Bible's prophesies, but I encourage you to discover them for yourself. If you want to understand Jesus' personal prophetic puzzle you need to have somewhat of an understanding on Bible prophecy.

Our prophetic puzzles come together as God builds our testimony through our life experiences, both the good and the bad. Our testimony makes up our individual prophetic puzzles, as well as the puzzle piece that goes into God's overall prophetic puzzle. The Spirit of prophecy weaves God's prophetic puzzle together. Our lives are puzzle pieces that connect God's puzzle together, just like all the characters we read about in the Bible. When God's puzzle comes together, it illuminates a picture of Jesus Christ. God sees us in His Son. It's like a giant puzzle of Jesus, but as we look closely, we realize that billions of other faces make up the picture. We are each one of those faces. Because our testimony is so important to our prophetic puzzle, let's look at the definition of the word *testimony*.

Testimony:

1. A solemn declaration usually made orally by a witness under oath in response to interrogation by a lawyer or authorized public official
2. Firsthand authentication of a fact: EVIDENCE
3. An outward sign
4. An open acknowledgment
5. A public profession of religious experience[1]

Positionally, we live under the new covenant of grace through faith in Jesus Christ. Relationally, we enter into the covenant and live it out daily. However, the devil preys on those who are unaware of the legal and spiritual truth of their salvation. He comes accusing us, condemning us, and seeking to keep us bound, but our testimony has the power to destroy every work of the enemy with the antidote, the blood of Jesus. As it says in Revelation:

"And they overcame him because of the blood of the Lamb and because of the word of their testimony, and they did not love their life even when faced with death" (Revelation 12:11 NASB1995).

Our testimony is compiled of many different parts, but it all started before the foundation of the earth. Those who choose Christ are His sheep, and they hear His voice. We are being drawn to Christ like a magnet to metal, and the pulling force is the Spirit of prophecy, the testimony of Jesus. When we are His, our lives are a walking sign pointing to Jesus. We are an acknowledgment of who He is, and our mouths speak forth all He has done for us. Our changed lives are evidence of our testimony. Jesus Christ is the most controversial figure that ever lived, and this is because He changed history, and our testimony is His story.

POEM: SOUND

I hear the trumpet of the Lord. The sound has been made clear. The alarm has been set. Come hither all you saints. It's time to gather and praise our king. Jesus sits on the throne. The throne of righteousness cries out. Come hear the call for the saints. Come up here and taste that the Lord is good.

A resounding call has been set. Do not delay or turn away. A sound of faith and courage has been brought forth. Come all you saints. The time is now.

The glory clouds are at hand. See them as the Holy Spirit grows. Feel the Spirit of the Lord as He searches for His remnant. All you saints come hear the call for the time of Jesus is now.

The hope of glory is the new sound. Prepare the way for the risen Lord. Listen for the trumpet. It's calling your name. Rise up! Rise up to the challenge. Fear not for the Lord is here. He takes a stand for us. Rise up to His calling for the gathering has begun. Come hither, you saints, and listen for the sound. The season has begun. The alarm has been set. Clear is the calling for those who wait upon the Lord.

- Ruthie Dickey

8

THE REVEALING

In the waiting season, everything about us is revealed, and most of all our character is revealed. To walk in our calling, we must allow God to expose the deepest parts of our hearts and purify them through obedience.

Often, this revealing of our character comes through trials and tribulations, which can give way to deep pain and sorrow. But we find hope and redemption as God reveals Himself to us. Redemption is a person—the person of Jesus—and He offers healing for our deep pain and sorrow. His healing in our lives strengthens our intimacy with Him, and He builds our trust for Him in our seasons of brokenness. In those seasons, we discover that everything we need is in Jesus. *In Him* is a spiritual place. That's why we pray *in Jesus' name.* A place exists in Him where we live and have our existence. Jesus is the door leading to the Father, and the Father gives us His soul, which I correlate to the Holy Spirit, who hovered over the vastness of the waters during creation. He is the one who searches the deep things of God and reveals His heart to us.

Emotions can lead us astray. Our hearts can deceive us. This is why we need to die to the flesh, the old ways, the old habits, the old thinking, the old man or woman, the things in childhood, the trauma, the abuse, the lies, the addictions. All of it needs to die with the devil. The devil is the author of killing, stealing, and destroying. So, when we come alive and are born again of water and the Spirit, we need to leave those things behind.

We are created in God's image and likeness. We are spirit (our inner being), soul (mind, will, and emotions), and body, which is the likeness of God. God is Spirit, the Holy Spirit is the soul of God, and Jesus Christ is the body (see 1 Thessalonians 5:23-24; Genesis 1:2-3; 1 Corinthians 2:9-16). When we receive Jesus, He makes us into a new creation. But we still need to learn to walk out our new identity in Him and rid ourselves of the old and sinful ways. This is why God reveals the depths of our hearts and calls us into purity.

REVEALING WHO WE ARE IN CHRIST

He is coming back for a bride (the church) without spot or wrinkle. In the waiting, we must allow God to remove any spots and wrinkles He finds in our lives so we can be holy as He is holy. We must listen closely as the whisper of the Holy Spirit reveals the mystery of His will for us. His will is found in understanding that He does the work as we yield to Him. We must forget about being perfect and, instead, let the mess of who we are unravel in the light of who He is. Christ in us is the hope of glory that we seek to walk in (see Colossians 1:27), and the waiting is the process of uncovering who we truly are in Him. We aren't the lies the devil whispers in our ears, and we aren't the past things we've done or encountered. We aren't the old person we were even yesterday. We are none of those things if we are in Him.

We will fly to new heights in the Spirit as we sit and get real with ourselves and God. He sees our nakedness, and He is waiting to clothe us with His light and cover us with His wings of protection. In the season of waiting, our desired perfection is already obtained, but we're waiting to walk into it fully. Jesus is knocking at the door of our hearts, and He wants to come in. We must let Him in today and ask Him for spiritual heart surgery. The spots and wrinkles are ironed out through the healing of the wounds. If we want to possess the treasures in the darkness, we must first give Him our whole hearts. We must allow Him to reveal what's in the dark. The treasures of darkness are things of God that He has not yet revealed to us. In the waiting, He reveals it all. As it says in Isaiah:

I will go before you and make the rough places smooth; I will shatter the doors of bronze and cut through their iron bars. I will give you the treasures of darkness and hidden wealth of secret places, so that you may know that it is I, the Lord, the God of Israel, who calls you by your name (Isaiah 45:2–3 NASB1995).

This verse gives us a perfect example of what the Lord does in heart surgery, which is what I call inner healing. He makes the rough patches smooth through the washing of the water of His word. He goes to great lengths to reach us and shatters every hindrance in the way. He cuts through the impossible and comforts the inconsolable.

Perhaps you have believed a lie about who God is, and you view Him through a broken lens of past hurts from strangers, family, friends, pastors, and others in ministry. You have blamed Him for the work of Satan. You have blamed Him for all the pain and suffering in the world, the death of your loved ones, the broken marriages, and the bondage in your kids' lives, but today I am exposing the liar, the devil who is the orchestrator of destruction. We must stop blaming God, recognize the work of Satan, and armor up to defeat him with the blood of Jesus. Jesus already defeated Satan. He's a defeated foe, but he will slither into the lives of those who are sleeping, and he will bite at unexpected times (see John 10:10). The good news is, Jesus has given us the keys to the kingdom and power over the enemy. We get to take hold of what's ours and attack.

MY SPIRITUAL HEART SURGERY

When we give God the broken pieces of our lives, He gives us a heart of gold to replace our heart of stone. In my life, this process began many years ago when I went into the spiritual place seated with Christ and saw the vision of myself in a hospital room on an operating table (as I mentioned previously in chapter 2). I was waiting for heart surgery, and Jesus was the doctor. I saw Jesus holding my heart. It looked like a real human heart, fully flesh. He took my heart out and washed it under water in the sink beside the hospital bed. This symbolized the washing of the water of the word (see Ephesians 5:26). As the water poured over my heart, I saw words supernaturally being inserted into my heart. These words were healing, prophecy, peace, love, and unity. As I gazed at my heart in amazement, I saw it turn to gold, and then Jesus placed it back into my chest. This is what it means to be seated with Christ in heavenly places—to say the kingdom of heaven is at hand.

This is a vivid picture of what it means to undergo heart surgery, or inner healing. An operating table is a place of transparency with God. It's a supernatural place where impossibilities become possible. In that place, God defies earthly realities and defines spiritual realities. For me, this part of the waiting involved getting to know God as the great physician, my heavenly surgeon.

RELEASING THE OLD AND LAYING HOLD OF THE NEW

In Ephesians 5, Paul describes Christ's goal for us:

…Christ also loved the church and gave Himself up for her, so that He might sanctify her, having cleansed her by the washing of water with the word, that He might present to Himself the church in all her glory, having no spot or wrinkle or any such thing; but that she would be holy and blameless (Ephesians 5:25–27 NASB1995).

Jesus isn't returning for a compromised, lukewarm, double-minded, or demonized bride (church). He's coming for one without spot or wrinkle, one who is set apart. Right now, as I write this book, it's nearing the end of the year 2023, representing a new era and new wine-skins. Jesus said, *"No one puts new wine into old wineskins; otherwise the wine will burst the skins, and the wine is lost and the skins as well; but one puts new wine into fresh wineskins" (Mark 2:22 NASB1995)*. It's time to let go of the old so the new wine can be poured in. It is time to deal with the things from our childhood, past traumas, bitterness, and unforgiveness. As we give God our broken pieces, the potter will produce His masterpieces out of us, the clay.

Many years ago, God spoke a prophetic word to me that I'm including below. If you believe it, you can receive it for yourself. Go ahead and take a bite of His goodness:

The Lord said, look around, My child. I'm everywhere. I will never leave you or forsake you. My word stands forever. The hope of your calling is being made known. The things of my nature are becoming your nature. Nothing can separate you from My love. Your hunger for Me is being filled. All who are thirsty will be given a drink. Rivers of living water are flowing out of your innermost being. Believe and open your eyes to a deeper understanding of Me. All mysteries are being revealed through My word. Like the waves of the sea is the motion I'm moving in your life. You will trust when you cannot see, and you will see Me, and you have seen who I am. You will know that I am God and will be made still. You will love like I love and see what I see. Your heart's desires will be filled, and your heart is a heart of gold. You've been made new. Your mind is of Mine. It's been renewed. Your family is made new. You are open to heaven, and My will is going to be done on earth as in heaven. Power beyond belief, My dear child. *Power.* You're learning about the enemy and that he's been defeated. He's not as big as he wants to appear. He trembles at you, because you are Mine. Your name is written in the book of life. You are individually special to Me. I know and care for you, and I know what you don't know about yourself. Your passion to help and heal others will be fulfilled through Me, Christ Jesus. The power that is coming is beyond imagination, it's here *now* and stirring up. You feel the stirring, and it's about to explode in a magnitude of ecstasy. Keep your eyes on the cross where salvation was bought. Your spirit's desire for souls to be saved was given to you by Me. Seek Me with open eyes and open heart. I'm way bigger than you can even believe.

MIRACLES REVEALED ALONG THE WAY

The waiting season of life isn't always a dry season of drought; in fact, the rain of His Spirit will drench our land with miracles along the way. The miracles revealed in the waiting are a mere taste of what's to come. I've seen so many miracles that I could write a book on them, but I'll share just a few here to encourage you. One major key to seeing and experiencing the miracles of God is to be a cheerleader for others. When we're in the waiting, we will see others who are in the winning, and when we do, we should cheer them on, knowing we all have a moment to shine with Christ. Each person's moment comes at exactly the right time (see 1 Thessalonians 5:23–24). Patience in the waiting will lead us into the promised land.

MY MOM'S MIRACLE

The most profound miracle in my waiting season was my mom's healing. I still wake up every day thanking God for doing the impossible. As I mentioned previously, her medical miracle came through deliverance, but after her miracle the Lord revealed why her healing process was so long. That said, I want to pull back those layers now so you can grab hold of this profound revelation. She was married to a man for thirty-five years, who was my adopted dad. They had retired and moved to Vegas to be by family, but she was deathly ill by this point. She felt as if she was being poisoned, and we believe she was. It was literally a life-or-death situation. While in Vegas she found out her husband was not who she thought he was, but out of honor for those involved, I will not go into those details. Furthermore, she knew she had to get on a plane and get back to Texas. So, she left her husband, came back home and never looked back.

When she came back to Texas after living in Vegas, she was dying. Her skin was yellowish, her blue veins were visible through her skin, and she weighed about 90 pounds. She was lifeless and confined in bed. I knew I needed to do something. I called on an old friend who believed in the full gospel and had the gift of healing. Even though I was skeptical of his beliefs, I had a feeling he might be able to help. He came over and prayed over her to be healed, and suddenly, the bed violently shook as her body straightened out before my eyes. She shouted out, "*I have no pain! I have no pain! Thank You, Jesus!*" She kept repeating it over and over. All was well as she was finally healed, or so I thought.

But after a year, she was in a worse condition than she'd been before. I sought the Lord, thinking, *I know You don't do incomplete work, so what is happening? How can she be sick again?* Not until a few years later did I receive the answer when we walked into a tent revival. The way I saw it, my options were either to plan her funeral or to get her to this revival. I don't even know the name of the evangelist who was speaking, which shows that a person's name doesn't have to be in lights or on TV in order to be used powerfully by God.

As my mom walked forward for prayer, she smelled a horrible stench of demons, but she didn't realize what it was at the time. The evangelist cast a spirit of infirmity out of her. She flipped and flopped back a few times and threw up demons for three days, but she's been healed ever since. That was almost seven years ago now.

I had finally received the answers I sought about why her previous healing hadn't lasted. When she received prayer, the healing power of God touched her body physically, but she wasn't healed spiritually. A spirit of infirmity (along with many other demons) was causing her physical issues. The root was spiritual, not physical. Thus, the demons within kept doing their work until she was worse than before. Some healings require deliverance. My mom's deliverance healing was life-changing for both of us. She went from death to life, which is why we have this ministry today.

THE COLORADO ROAD MIRACLE

Another miracle happened on a Colorado road while on a girls' trip with an old friend who was just starting to seek God. I was still in the revealing and cleansing process, but God was building His fire inside me daily. As we drove along, we decided to take a shortcut on a back road, but as we drove, the mud on the road got thicker, and we got stuck. We also had no cell phone service, and the gas light was about to come on. I told her we should pray and God would help us out. A few minutes after we prayed, a truck appeared, and two men said to follow them. I had worked with a stick to get some of the mud off the tires, and to my surprise, we suddenly became unstuck. It was supernatural. We followed this truck up a road and found ourselves back on the main highway. I believe those men may have been angels. We still had one problem. On the main highway, the next gas station, according to the GPS, was still miles away, and the gas light had been on for a while. I prayed again, and suddenly we saw a gas station up the road—a gas station not listed on the GPS. I'll never forget that day and what God did for us. Not only did He help us out, but He also showed Himself faithful to my friend who wasn't yet a strong believer. That event set her on fire for Jesus.

ANGELS REVEALED IN FLASHING LIGHTS

Sometimes we get to go to mountain peaks in the valley of the waiting. The mountain-peak moments are the ones that keep our spirits hiking for more. One ordinary day, my mom and I were doing a deliverance prayer meeting with a woman when, in a vision, I saw three angels walk in the front door. I said, "The angels are here."

We continued to pray while our ministry patient had her eyes closed. Suddenly, a big flash of light came from behind me, and our patient opened her eyes. I said, "Did you see that?"

She said, "Yes, I saw a big flash of light with my eyes closed." Then, while our eyes were still open, another lightning flash shot right before our eyes. We will never forget that moment and believe the flashes of lights were God's angels. She and I still talk about it.

ON A SPIRITUAL MISSION AT MY NEIGHBOR'S HOUSE

I love it when God takes over a ministry session, like when He sent me to a neighbor. This neighbor was very special to me because the Lord had called me to minister to her uniquely. She is the apple of His eye. He has His mind on her, and I'm the God-agent sent in her path. What an honor it is to be used by God. One day she texted me that she was ready for more of Jesus and deliverance prayer. Those are the kind of words that send me running. Another of my neighbors also came along. We went to her house and prepped for the glory of the Lord, because we knew this was a holy moment in time.

We needed to change the atmosphere in the home, so we told the Alexa unit to play "This is How I Fight My Battles" by Michael W. Smith, but instead, it played "I Can Only Imagine" by Mercy Me. We knew this was the Lord's doing because of the tears streaming down my neighbor's face. Her ex-boyfriend, with whom she had a child, had died, and that song was played at his funeral. I knew God was taking us back to this memory of her life so that He could heal her wounds. I held her as we both cried and prayed. Then suddenly she said, "Who are you? Who are you? All I see is a light around you."

I told her it was God. She said she saw an angel. Meanwhile, my other neighbor was praying over the house and casting out demons. Suddenly, the living room filled with a glorious light. God had taken over, and the house was clean. May God do the same in your life.

THE CLOUD OF HIS GLORY REVEALED TO ME

When we walk with Christ, He will use us for divine interruptions that bring forth His glory, just like he did when I was sent to my neighbors house. Not long ago, the glory cloud followed me to my little church in Andrews, Texas. As I preached one Sunday morning, the fire of God hit my tongue and pierced those in the audience. Afterward, I prophesied over a few people, but I never imagined what would come from that morning.

A few weeks later, one of the girls I had prophesied over called me. She told me that when I was preaching that Sunday she had seen a cloud around me. She also told me she had had a dream the previous night, and after the dream, the glory of the Lord and His presence filled the place where she was staying. She said, in this dream, she was taken down a long, dark hallway to a door with a beaming light coming underneath the door frame. When she opened the door, she saw me standing in a cloud of foggy glory, and I said, "You have witnessed a miracle of God."

A few days later, she began to be attacked by the enemy at night, so we set up a prayer session. We walked her through the spiritual cleansing of the home she was living in, throwing away occult items that were inviting demonic spirits. Through this process, the fire of God fell upon her, and she was changed. She said it was life-changing to experience the presence of God so strongly. The glory cloud then filled my house, and she could see it through Facetime video on the phone. I don't know what happened to this girl, but I do know that no matter where she's at in life, God's glory is chasing her down. I am so thankful to have been the vessel God used to touch her.

HE GAVE ME FAVOR WITH AN ATHEIST

The glory of the Lord is so strong that He will even cause atheists to be at peace with us. God has told me He has His eye on a man I know through social media. The Lord gave me a mandate to minister to this man, and I've been doing so for a few years. One day, when I shared with him a little glimpse of my testimony, he wrote, "I'm speechless; I'm shocked. Actually, you are a true Christian, and I don't even like to call you that; you're a true woman of God." Now, this man doesn't like Christians and has turned away from them, yet he recognized something mighty at work in my life. Even an atheist spoke blessings over my life. I pray this friend reads this book and the glory of God's presence overtakes him, for he has been hand-picked by God and is part of my earthy assignment.

MY DESTINY REVEALED IN DREAMS

I'm a visionary Seer and a dreamer. I have visions while I'm awake and sometimes up to three dreams a night. Dreams are a different realm in which our spirit is active, and God desires to interact with us in dreams just like he did with King Solomon. He visited him in a dream, and it changed the course of his destiny and the nation. That said, my next book will be on dreams, but I want to share one particular dream with you now.

It all began on a porch swing, where I would meet with the Holy Spirit. I couldn't see Him, but I felt Him, and I heard Him speak. He spoke telepathically to me. When we would rock on the swing, together we would launch into a new place through spiritual translation. When you're translated in the Spirit you go from one place to another instantly. I remember I was hovering over the ocean, and it was slightly scary because it seemed so real, but I knew I was safe. Again, we would be back on the swing and in a flash, I'd be translated to a new place. This time I was in someone's house. I was on assignment to pray over their home and for the people living there. Next, I was in a place with the late Derek Prince, who I quoted previously. For those of you know don't know the name Derek Prince, he was a profound deliverance minister, and is still considered a past general in the faith today. In the dream he spoke with me about the hardships of ministry, and then he handed me a white horse head statue and told me to carry on the work of deliverance. Then I woke up.

Something amazing happened the next day to confirm the authenticity of the dream. I walked into a store and there was the same horse head statue I was handed in my dream. I bought the statue, and it sits on my desk as a prophetic reminder of my assignment in the Lord and that he is with me. Through the revealing process of the waiting anything is possible, and I encourage you to wait with expectancy.

POEM: NORTH

You are my dwelling place. When my heart is heavy, I seek You.
I drink Your fragrance of love.
Fill me with Your presence so I may find peace.
Peace, peace, come upon me.
Drench me with Your love.
Show me the hope of You.

I fear and tremble at Your gates.
You are the one and true God.
Help me see through the turmoil.

Guide my path to righteousness.
I fear not for the tribulation is near
You are the only one truth.
You are the north that I seek.
God, my God, You are my refuge.
Your love conquers all.

- Ruthie Dickey

9

PERSEVERING IN THE WAITING

One essential component of the season of waiting is growing in our intimacy with God. Our relationship with Him matters so much more than anything we accomplish for Him. So often we want to get ahead and do things our way. We want to do great things for God and be known and recognized. But our spirit knows what we really need. Our spirit wants to be in communion with God. We think we know what's best and how it all should work out, but in the waiting, we find out how much more we have to learn.

I've found that God's invitation to wait on Him is about slowing me down, allowing me to get frustrated enough to stop and ask questions. Questions like, *Why isn't what You said happening already?* Through this frustration I learned that I had put certain expectations on God. I wanted things to go a certain way. I learned, it's good to expect God to move on my behalf, but I can't put specific expectations on how He does it. If we will trust God to help us fulfill our destiny no matter how it looks, then we will bypass being disappointed when things don't go our way. Really, the waiting is all about being wholly undone so His will can be done. The undoing has much to do with our mindsets, which are limited to our human intellect, theology, culture, upbringing, and society. As we encounter life, our minds often get filled with the debris that the wind of the world blows in. That's why Jesus told us to build our lives on the rock, not the sand:

Everyone then who hears these words of mine and does them will be like a wise man who built his house on the rock. And the rain fell, and the floods came, and the winds blew and beat on that house, but it did not fall, because it had been founded on the rock. And everyone who hears these words of mine and does not do them will be like a foolish man who built his house on the sand. And the rain fell, and the floods came, and the winds blew and beat against that house, and it fell, and great was the fall of it (Matthew 7:24–27 ESV).

When the wind comes, the house built with sand is scattered and destroyed, but a house on the rock stands firm. The sand is the thoughts in our minds; when the wind of life comes, suddenly our minds are running all over the place in a million pieces. However, when we build our house on the rock, we are unshakeable and strong when the wind blows. The *rock* is the solid foundation of Christ and His mind. If we want to be joined to Him and have the mind of Christ, our human minds must yield. As we continue to yield throughout the years, I believe our minds fuse together with the mind of Christ like a solid rock.

The waiting is a divine season of preparation. So many people give up in the waiting right before the breakthrough. I have been tempted to give up several times, but the Holy Spirit has always counseled me through the doubts. God has also given me good friends who have lifted me up and helped me to see clearly when the fog has rolled in. The waiting is something we must choose. It's easy to want to jump ahead or try to make things happen, but when we do that, we miss out on the spiritual training needed to carry us to the finish line. We can actually take a major detour in our destiny by avoiding the waiting.

WORKING OUT IN THE SPIRITUAL GYM

The waiting is like a spiritual gym, and the Holy Spirit is our personal trainer. We don't get fit overnight. It takes time, dedication, listening, focusing, habit change, and diet change. The diet change is where we become more hungry for God than we do for anything else. We learn to eat His flesh, which is the bread of life. His flesh is the word manifested, the spiritual manna from heaven that we digest into our whole beings. We drink His blood, which is the covenant we live by; it's life and death. We choose to not love our lives, even when faced with death, because we know the blood has authority over death. In fact, in Christ we don't experience death, but life to everlasting life.

In this gym, we learn to lay down everything we are to become everything He is. As we eat His flesh and drink His blood, we soon realize how malnourished we have been. We recognize that the waiting isn't merely us waiting on Him, but He is actually also waiting on us.

God gave Jeremiah a word that applies to us, too:

The word that came to Jeremiah from the Lord: "Arise, and go down to the potter's house, and there I will let you hear my words." So I went down to the potter's house, and there he was, working at his wheel. And the vessel he was making of clay was spoiled in the potter's hand, and he reworked it into another vessel, as it seemed good to the potter to do. Then the word of the Lord came to me: "O house of Israel, can I not do with you as this potter has done?" declares the Lord. "Behold, like the clay in the potter's hand, so are you in my hand, O house of Israel" (Jeremiah 18:1–6 ESV).

Throughout life, we pick up garbage and allow it to form strongholds in our minds. We harbor wounds in our hearts and sometimes even shelter demons in our spiritual house; therefore, the Lord looks at us and sees His artwork defected. He made us perfect before the earth's foundation, but sin and iniquity put stains on us.

Yes, Jesus died and rose again so we can walk in His holiness and righteousness. He took all the curses on the cross. He bought salvation for us all with His blood. His blood is the ultimate authority. However, we must choose all of Him to receive all we want from Him. We are a spiritual house, and when we accept Jesus, we sign our home over to Him. Our spirit is made new and perfect. But we still have cabinets and closets in our souls (mind, will, and emotions) that are full of darkness and spider webs. We often don't even know they exist because we have forgotten. Or we pretend it's all okay because we'd rather not go there.

Jesus, the cornerstone on which the house was built, wants to take up residence in every dark place and bring His light. The waiting is all about letting Him into those places. We want His glory, His presence, His nature, His love, His spiritual gifts, and everything else good, but with our hearts and minds, we choose something else, something less than. Salvation is for all, but not all choose it. Jesus broke the curses for us, but we must enforce His righteousness within the spiritual realm of our lives.

We choose all of Him by working out in the spiritual gym in the waiting. It's all about yielding—what we are willing to let go of and what we are ready to relinquish. He will replace and refill those places with His light and love. One of the biggest hindrances to this is pride. In the waiting, we must be willing to crush everything that crawls out from the dark—and we must do it immediately.

EATING CAKE WITH JESUS

For example, in the waiting, we experience immense warfare in the mind. We have to choose between the worldly ways and the broad roads of destruction or the narrow road that leads to eternal life. We must decide which master we will serve. We can't have our cake and eat it too. That's how it works with the world. The prince of the air is Satan, and he will put a delicious cake in front of us, but if we eat it, we will feel sick. On the other hand, Jesus gives us cake and even adds sprinkles on top. He takes His time on it, making it look exquisite. Jesus is not in a rush, because He knows what He is doing, and He knows it's worth the wait. When it's finally ready, He will give us the cake and tell us to give some away to others. We will eat just the right amount, get satisfied, and bring joy to others as they sit at the table and eat with us. The cake Satan gives us is counterfeit. It looks so good, like God's cake, but with no sprinkles. It was made fast and easy, leading those who eat it to have regrets.

When eating cake, we must look to the baker and look at the source behind the offer. Do we want the first cake now, or would we rather wait? It all comes down to what Paul the apostle wrote in Romans:

I appeal to you, therefore, brothers, by the mercies of God, to present your bodies as a living sacrifice, holy and acceptable to God, which is your spiritual worship. Do not be conformed to this world, but be transformed by the renewal of your mind, that by testing you may discern what is the will of God, what is good and acceptable and perfect (Romans 12:1–2 ESV).

All of heaven is appealing to us to offer up a living sacrifice. We don't do this on the altar in a church with animals; all of that has passed away. Now we offer up a daily sacrifice and build an altar to God in our hearts. That's why inner healing is so important—so we can offer what's acceptable to God. We need everything to be undone in us so Jesus can manifest through us. We give up our bodies as our own and offer them as spiritual homes for God. Our bodies were created by Him and made for Him so that the King of Glory may come in.

Who is this King of Glory? The Lord, strong and mighty, the Lord, mighty in battle! Lift up your heads, O gates! And lift them up, O ancient

doors, that the King of glory may come in. Who is this King of Glory?
The Lord of hosts, he is the King of glory! Selah (Psalms 24:8-10
ESV).

Our minds are housed in our heads, and our heads are the gate through which the Lord wants to come in so that we can be transformed. The ancient key and doorway to transformation comes by renewing the mind (see Ephesians 4:23–24). Our minds can be made new. Our minds can be restored. Our minds can recover lost memory, and the dull areas can be injected with brilliance. We as humans have a will, God has a will, and Satan has a will, so to discern the perfect will of God, we must dismantle the cunning will of Satan. This all starts in the mind. Once the mind is renewed, the body becomes a house of prayer—a sanctuary for the lost and a secret place like the Holy of Holies where our spirit is one with God.

In the waiting, the Lord deals with the mind. He also pinpoints the motives of the heart where wickedness is stored and plucks out every splinter. When the heart has wickedness, this wickedness is pushed into a filing cabinet in our minds. We can know what's truly in our hearts and minds by what comes out of our mouths. As Jesus said, *"The good person out of the good treasure of his heart produces good, and the evil person out of his evil treasure produces evil, for out of the abundance of the heart his mouth speaks"* (Luke 6:45 ESV).

To be transformed by the renewing of the mind, we must read the Bible and meditate on it, not rush through it. We must sit with the Holy Spirit as He teaches it to us. This is a type of schooling that no Bible college can give us. In fact, many Bible colleges throw out the mind of Christ and teach out of human wisdom. I've found, if we want to be transformed, we must unlearn much of what we thought we knew. The closer I get to God, the less I know, because His rivers of revelation are vast. As soon as I think I'm swimming in the rivers with excellence, a new current shifts me in a new direction. God always has more. Once we learn what He's saying, we can pass and go to the next level of glory.

REST IN THE LORD

In the waiting, we enter into a refreshing rest. As we rest in Christ, we feel lighter because we are unbecoming everything not of our original design, unlearning all the lies we've been told about God, and allowing the Holy Spirit to undo the things that hold us back.

One day, in February 2021, as I sat in bed, the voice of the Lord began to flow out of my mouth with the most beautiful words. His words of revelation were enlightening, bringing a more profound rest into my whole being. Here is what He spoke to me:

Tell my people to find their rest in Me. We all hear the phrase *"rest in the Lord,"* but rest is complete trust. Without complete trust in the Lord, there is no rest. Coupled with trust must be strong faith. You have faith knowing your Daddy will work it all out. That He has your back. When you enter a place where complete trust and faith combine as two rivers flowing as one, you reach the threshold of rest, and the result is abiding. This is what it means to abide in Me. Read the word, allow the Holy Spirit to teach you all things, and trust in His ways. This requires a cleaning of the heart and a renewing of the mind. We all need transformation, which comes by renewing the mind. Be renewed in the spirit of your mind. Next is the transfiguration, where you are abiding in Him. He is in you. It's Him doing it all. As you yield your vessel of dust, He will fill it with His glory.

PROMOTION IN THE WAITING

As we find our rest in God, our identity—who we are in Him—washes away all insecurity. We become whole and healthy spiritually. Spiritual health leads to mental and physical health. If you're not well mentally or physically, it's time to target what's going on spiritually. In the waiting, the Lord deals with this and teaches us to become *one in spirit* with Him. As we dive in and remain teachable, we will become usable by God. He will open doors of promotion in the waiting.

In my waiting season, people asked me to do revivals, to preach at churches, to teach for ministry institutes, to appear on several podcasts, to help on prophetic prayer teams, and to minister on television. I don't say this to boast, but to encourage you. Even in the waiting, we experience open doors. With each opportunity, I had a choice to become full of myself or full of Him. It's possible to get opportunities by bragging and boasting. I've seen many people do this. Eventually, those who do this end up being lone wolves. We don't want to make our own doors, but wait for God's. The more doors God opens, the more I realize I need Him. No one needs to hear another man-made sermon or another feel-good revival message. It may be exciting for a night, but tomorrow nothing has changed. No one needs a prophetic word full of emptiness with sugar on top. No one needs to sit through another self-help class, but we do need God to show up and show off. And we do need Him—and Him alone—to receive the glory.

HE SHOWED UP

A few years ago, our ministry hosted a woman's retreat in Ruidoso, New Mexico. People attended from various areas in Texas, and some even flew in from New York. Many were expecting a mighty move of God, including me. However, as the one who was hosting the presence of God, I felt a lot of pressure. On the first night, before we began, I went into the bathroom and prayed this prayer to God: "Lord, all of these women are here for You. I'm here for You, and I can do nothing without You. Despite me, Lord, please do something." Oh yes, God definitely did something. The oil of gladness fell upon the ladies, and everyone was filled with the Lord's joy and the Holy Spirit's laughter. Many were slain by the Spirit of God, and the rest were filled with His peace. A vast cloud hovered directly over the building we were staying in—a bright white cloud with nothing else around just hovering over us. When we talked about angels, shooting stars appeared in the night sky. The presence of the Lord was thick.

Many women were restored at this retreat, including me. I didn't know it then, but the prayer I prayed that night would become a lifelong prayer. I say it before everything I am called to do. No one needs to see or hear me, but we all need a fresh touch of the presence of God. The presence of God is what changes the lives of others. The presence of God is what sustains the life of others. The presence of God can hit people suddenly like a bolt of lightning, placing the fire of God within their innermost being. And just like that, hell lost another one.

POEM: HOPE

Hope is upon us.
Where is the Lord?
The Lord is beside us.
Let hope arise.
Let faith ring clear.

His hope is in you.
You are His dwelling place.
Let hope arise.

Let the Lord ring clear.
He is and was and is to come.
Let no one despair.
Hope is what we crave.
His hope is what we receive.

Let not the enemy come upon you.
His grace is here.
Do you not perceive it.

May truth arise.
May glory come forth.
The time is now.

Let hope arise.
Let the day of the Lord ring clear.
Holy, holy, holy is His name.

- Ruthie Dickey

10

CONSIDER IT ALL JOY WHEN YOU FACE TRIALS

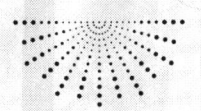

Consider it all joy, my brethren, when you encounter various trials, knowing that the testing of your faith produces endurance. And let endurance have its perfect result, so that you may be perfect and complete, lacking in nothing (James 1:2–4 NASB1995).

The trials of life come to us all, whether we are saved or unsaved. With Christ, we can overcome as He did. Without Christ, we are trampled underfoot. Sometimes, even though we are saved, we may still feel depressed, which is a sign we need a fresh filling. When we die to the flesh, we come alive in the spirit. We experience ecstatic joy when we are alive in the spirit. We must focus, therefore, on things of the spirit. *We must starve the flesh and feed the spirit.* When we starve the flesh—our human desires that are full of lustful passions—we feed the spirit. When we feed the spirit, we are in the process of becoming one with the Holy Spirit.

It's the same concept as God's ideal for biblical marriage, "....*it's not good for man to be alone*" *(Genesis 2:18 NIV)*. God created man and woman to have communion and companionship with each other. They worked together to fulfill a purpose. God created the heavens and the earth and wanted humans to have dominion over His creation. When He created Adam, He breathed into his nostrils, and that breath became life. The breath of God is Spirit, and His Spirit gives us life. We have power in our breath to breathe forth life or death. When we speak out His word and align with Him, we have unity in our spirits, which are joined to the Holy Spirit. We become one with God when we align with Him. It's a co-laboring relationship. We work in partnership with God; we yield to Him as He moves through us. This is what God desires for marriage as well, and this is why we are called His bride. He wants a relationship with us.

A STORY BY SMITH WIGGLESWORTH

In this relationship, under the new covenant, we are seated in heavenly places with Christ. This is the truth about our positioning in Him, but to see the fruit of this, we must do our part relationally. We have free will and must choose daily to deny the will of the flesh and to engage with the will of Christ. Our flesh must be crucified with Christ. Accepting Christ isn't an idea; it's an action. We must take our cross all the way to Calvary and die to our flesh so that Christ's will can be made manifest. A story in a book by Smith Wigglesworth explains this analogy perfectly:

A young monk came one day to his father superior and asked, *"Father, what is it to be dead to self?"*

The father replied, "I cannot explain it now; but I have a duty for you to perform. Brother Martin died last week and is buried in the churchyard of our order. Go to his grave, standing close beside it, repeat in a loud voice all the good things you ever heard of him. After this, say all the flattering things you can invent, and attribute to him every saintly grace and virtue without regard to truth, and report the result to me."

The young monk went to do his bidding, wondering what all this could mean. Soon he returned, and the father asked him what had transpired. "Why, nothing," replied the young man. "I did as you told me, and that was all."

"Did Brother Martin make no reply?" asked the superior.

"Of course, he did not, for he was dead," said the monk.

The elder shook his head thoughtfully, saying, "That is very strange. Go again tomorrow at the same hour, and repeat at the graveside all the evil you ever heard concerning Brother Martin. Add to that the worst slander and calumny your mind can imagine and report the result to me."

Again, the young man obeyed and brought back the same report. He had heaped unlimited abuse on the head of Brother Martin and yet had received no reply.

"From Brother Martin, you may learn," said the father, "what it is to be dead to self." Neither flattery nor abuse has moved him, for he is dead. So, the disciple who is dead to self will be insensible to these things, hearing neither voice of praise nor retaliation, but all personal feeling will be lost in the service of Christ."[1]

We need to reach a place where we lay aside all people-pleasing and all self-pleasing, getting rid of every idol in our hearts that takes room from the Holy Spirit. This often requires us to go through inner healing and deliverance. As we read the word of God and allow His words to marinate deep within our souls, we will experience the renewing of the mind, which leads to our transfiguration (when people see Christ in us). As we fall in love with Jesus, our desires shift and align with His desires for our lives. We then want to align with what Psalms 139 says—that He has written out our days. Our obedience springs forth from a deep well of divine love and flows like a river, and that river is a representation of the Holy Spirit. The evidence is the fruit of the Spirit. This is His fruit, not ours. It doesn't come through works or effort; it comes by transformation (renewing the mind) and transfiguration (when people see Christ in us).

Let's examine some of the fruit of the Spirit.

DIVINE LOVE

Love is such a profound mystery that it has been at the center of cultural attention since the beginning of time. Unfortunately, our culture is repeating history and has come under a spell of witchcraft (through Ishtar), which has caused the perversion of authentic love. Love is a basic human need, so understanding true love is essential. If we encounter counterfeit love, our primary needs will not be met, and we will experience a void in our souls, which the enemy will try to enter and fill if we allow him.

To understand what love is, we must also understand what it's not. We will be deceived if we look at the worldly definition of love. To know what love is, we must look at who God is. We hear the catchphrase, "*Love is love,*" but that's not true. God is love. Love in itself is not a god, but God is love. Love is not a sexual act, a feeling, or a phrase. Love is a person; love through Christ is the most powerful force alive. Love is the light of Christ. Love isn't something you do. Although love does have action, true love is the Holy Spirit possessing us.

When it comes to love, we can't fake it until we make it. Love is either real or fake. Sure, we can try to manufacture love, but eventually, the facade comes crumbling down. That's why we must not look at outward appearances or expressions but must discern the spirit behind a person.

I used to always pray, "God, let Your Holy Spirit fill me to overflowing with His love so that I can genuinely love others how You do. I don't want it to be something I try to do. I want it to be who I am because it's who You are. So Holy Spirit, I ask You to possess me with Your love."

This may sound extreme to some, but the choice to allow spirits that are not of God to possess parts of our soul is even more extreme.

The Bible tells us that love is self-sacrificing:

"For God so loved the world that He gave His only begotten Son, that whoever believes in Him should not perish but have everlasting life" (John 3:16).

Just one drop of Jesus' blood is sufficient to replace a thousand worldly things we gave up to follow Him. His love is intoxicating, everlasting, and has the power to cover a multitude of sins. No sin can stand in the way of the love of Christ. As Paul wrote:

Love suffers long and is kind; love does not envy; love does not parade itself, is not puffed up; does not behave rudely, does not seek its own, is not provoked, thinks no evil; does not rejoice in iniquity, but rejoices in the truth; bears all things, believes all things, hopes all things, endures all things (1 Corinthians 13:4–7).

When we read these verses, we can clearly see that no one but Jesus could ever truly walk in this kind of love. That is why we have the Holy Spirit. He fills us up daily and loves others through us. This is how the Holy Spirit works. When we yield, He fills, flows, and moves through us supernaturally.

Keep in mind that love also disciplines and rebukes. Correction is part of real love; we willfully receive correction when we love God. Only pride stands in the way of godly discipline. We see this clearly in Jesus' words to the churches in Revelation:

As many as I love, I rebuke and chasten. Therefore be zealous and repent. Behold, I stand at the door and knock. If anyone hears My voice and opens the door, I will come in to him and dine with him, and he with Me (Revelation 3:19-20).

God loves us, so He will rebuke us. The question is not *if it will happen*, but *what* you will do when it does. The key is to repent, turn away from sin, and listen. When we hear the voice of God, He is opening the door and inviting us to sit and eat at His table. But if we can't take correction, we can't experience real love.

The greatest commandment is to love God with our whole being and to love our neighbors as ourselves. In order to abide by God's word, we must first be delivered from everything inside us that isn't of God. That's why deliverance is so important. To love God is to walk in humility, recognizing we won't understand everything along the way. When we love God, we build an altar in our hearts for Him. If we love God first, He will love others through us. That's how we are able to love our neighbors as ourselves. God is love, so He is the standard of love. We must follow Christ as Lord and receive the Holy Spirit in order to love God effectively. His Holy Spirit moves through us, producing supernatural fruit that we as humans can't obtain alone. As He moves through us, only then can we minister that love back to our Father. God's love is extraordinarily supernatural. It doesn't come from us, but is available to us and can flow through us.

If you live in darkness, the love of God will shine a light exposing it so that you can expel it and come up higher with Him, to where you're positioned. Remember, you're in heavenly places with Christ positionally, but darkness hinders your relationship with Him. Real love exposes darkness; it never conforms to it. God's love sets a standard. To the world, having a standard of holiness is hate; that's the mass deception of our culture today. If we love our neighbor, we shine a light on the darkness.

FINDING PURE JOY IN TRIALS

The joy of the Lord comes from being filled with the Holy Spirit. We have a choice to be continually filled with the Holy Spirit every day. When we face trials, we have a choice to make. Will we turn to God in faith and persevere, or will we forfeit our joy before the breakthrough? The key is to have joy during the trials. This sort of joy is definitely supernatural. It's impossible in our own efforts. Jesus wants us to lay our lives at the altar and allow Him to carry the weight of the burdens while healing the sting of the pain. The trials teach us to lean into God and obey Him in order to see the best results. Trials shape our destiny, leaving us with a choice to press in or get run over. Trials test our allegiance to God. We develop a close friendship with the Holy Spirit by allowing Him to fight our battles.

One major trial was when I moved locations a few years ago because I heard the Lord calling me to make a change. Although I didn't understand everything, I packed my bags, sold my house, and moved forty miles away to a little town decorated with dirt, tumbleweeds, and farm animals. I was so excited to see what God would do. I knew I had been sent as a pioneer in the land to host revivals. My mandate was all of West Texas, but this town would be my home for a while. Unfortunately, as soon as I moved, I came face-to-face with betrayal, manipulation, and witchcraft in the least expected places. The opposition that comes with pioneering can feel like a dark hallway, with voices murmuring all around, but as we keep our eyes focused on the light, the fruit of God's Spirit will begin to sprout.

PERFECT PEACE

For much of my life, peace felt far from me. In fact, it seemed like peace was running in the opposite direction. For a time, I even became comfortable in chaos because it was familiar. I didn't know it was actually a familiar spirit tethered to my bloodline, but I did recognize that fighting against it seemed impossible. And it was impossible until God broke down the iron bars that were keeping my soul trapped in captivity. Before my God invasion, the concept of peace seemed like a fairytale. However, after I received God's peace, I appreciated it so greatly because I knew what it was like to live in the presence of deep darkness.

Throughout my personal journey of waiting, I realized that

peace is a supernatural substance that radiates from Jesus Christ. Jesus is the prince of peace (see Isaiah 9:6). This is such a profound reality. When I experience peace, I know He is in my mist. Authentic peace cannot be obtained outside of Jesus Christ. Yes, people do seek out counterfeit peace through New Age practices, meditation, and drug use. The people who do these things are striving to find peace, but real peace is a presence that invades our hearts because of grace.

One time, in the early years of our marriage, my husband and I were having a heated argument, and I was angry. When he left the house, I thought to myself all the things I could say, because I was determined to win the argument. The Holy Spirit then told me to humble myself, but I was stubborn. I felt I had to get the last word. I was prepared to unleash my fury on my husband as soon as he walked in the door, but instead, I was divinely interrupted by the conquering presence of the prince of peace. The peace of God filled our kitchen and stopped us both in our tracks.

We sat in silence, and I said, "Do you feel that?"

My husband said, "Yes," and the argument was immediately over.

Years before this, I had spent much time seeking God daily, and because of this, He was welcome to invade my space. Even in our weakest moments, drops of God's glory will manifest through the fruit of the Holy Spirit. Peace is a powerful remedy when people want you to rage. Through pruning and yielding, I learned it's better to have peace than to prove who's right. The more I read the word of God and unify with Christ, the living word, the more the fruit of peace is able to grow within. As Paul wrote:

Rejoice in the Lord always. Again I will say, rejoice! Let your gentleness be known to all men. The Lord is at hand. Be anxious for nothing, but in everything by prayer and supplication, with thanksgiving, let your requests be made known to God; and the peace of God, which surpasses all understanding, will guard your hearts and minds through Christ Jesus (Philippians 4:4-7).

WAITING PATIENTLY

At one time in my life, just the thought of waiting patiently made me want to hurry all the more. My mind goes about a hundred miles a minute, so by nature I'm fast paced. I'm one who is ready to run the marathon for Christ and jump the hurtles; however, as the Lord slowed me down, my revelation of His ways became clearer. Going from point A to point Z isn't beneficial if I miss all the steps in between. Waiting patiently is all about the process God takes us through. In that process, we learn that the best place to be is at Jesus' feet.

Learning patience was one of my hardest struggles, yet yielding to the Holy Spirit in this area preserved me in many ways. I'm prophetic by nature. I was born that way, and I function in that office. I'm always looking to the future, seeing what's to come, planning revival, and teaching classes on the gifts of the Spirit. Because of this, I'm eager to just jump ahead and see the manifestation of what the Lord has shown. Yet often, a profound period of time exists between a prophetic word and its manifestation. Personally pioneering prophetic words involves breaking up ground during the in-between stages of the overall fulfillment. In other words, it's a process that can't just be jumped over. In these waiting periods, I have learned to lean into the Holy Spirit so He can fill me afresh with supernatural patience.

I've learned (and I'm still learning) not to jump ahead. I'm learning to praise Him along the way, mountain high or valley low, because He deserves my praise at every step of the process. In the waiting, as I have climbed each mountain, faced life lessons, and received deliverance, He has brought me into deep levels of heart healing I didn't even know I needed. For years I have watched people take off in ministry very quickly, especially on social media, but their character was cringeworthy. Because of what I saw, I thank the Lord for the waiting in my own life. I could have been one of those people if I had knocked down doors the Lord hadn't given me the keys to yet. The Lord desires to give us opportunities to partner with Him, but waiting patiently is about trusting His timing for promotion. If we are always asking others to bring us into their churches, organizations, or spaces, we are not waiting on the Lord.

KINDNESS MATTERS

When we clothe ourselves with kindness, we are releasing a supernatural, life-altering substance. Trauma can build up strong walls, but kindness can tear them down. Kindness can turn a hard heart into a soft heart. Kindness is a weapon of warfare against the enemy at work in people.

Kindness is fueled by compassion. When we have compassion, we understand people's emotional needs, and when we have kindness, we respond to those needs with action. Kindness and compassion work together to bring love and peace into people's lives. Kindness is an antidote to diffuse negative situations. In the Oxford dictionary, the definition of *antidote* is "a medicine taken or given to counteract a particular poison." Through the working of the Holy Spirit, we are able to give what is good to others in return for evil. This breaks down our natural, fleshly response, which is to return evil for evil. Kindness breaks the barriers of evil. This is the principle at work in Proverbs 25:21–22: *"If your enemy is hungry, give him bread to eat, and if he is thirsty, give him water to drink, for you will heap burning coals on his head, and the Lord will reward you" (ESV).*

The fruit of kindness comes with great responsibility and requires obedience to God. We must make sure we are walking with the fruit of the Holy Spirit and not operating out of a wound or an ulterior motive. To find the root of the operation of kindness we must examine our hearts. To examine our hearts, we must listen to the words coming out of our mouths. The mouth tells the motives of the heart (see Matthew 12:34–37). I have heard people say things like, "The kindest people are always the loneliest," or, "Kind people do everything for others, but no one does anything for them." These kinds of statements illuminate an inner wound, showing us that their kindness toward others is motivated by an attempt to meet the need of their wound. The kindness given by the Holy Spirit comes from a healed heart and a clear vision of the heart of the Father. God will show us situations in which kindness is the antidote that will manifest His kingdom. God rewards kindness, and sometimes God will use people to reward another person's kindness, but we must always keep our focus on God. He is the one we look to for reward and approval.

The kingdom of darkness seeks to prey upon people who are naturally compassionate and kind in order to take advantage of them. When the fruit of kindness comes from the Holy Spirit, the kingdom of darkness is dismantled, not empowered. The Holy Spirit knows what aspect of His fruit is needed to nourish any given situation, and if we obey Him, we see results. Sometimes the situation calls for correction, which is a fruit of love rather than an act of kindness. For example, if someone is always calling you for money, you may think it's compassionate and kind to give them all your money, when in fact it's a demon in them taking advantage of you. The proper fruit may be saying *no* (self-control) and talking to them about changing their lifestyle (correction through love).

THE GOODNESS OF GOD

The goodness of God is a hard subject for many, especially when they read the Old Testament. In the New Testament, it's easier for people to see the goodness of God through the sacrificial love of Jesus. People often struggle to see the goodness of God because they have a filter over their eyes that magnifies the negative. They are looking from the earthy view instead of the heavenly view. The heavenly view comes through the eyes of Christ. The earthly view comes from Satan.

I don't teach people to think positively while ignoring the truth. I don't tell them to live in la-la land and ignore historical facts or science. Instead, I call people to enter into a real relationship with God, which comes only through His son, Jesus. In my studies I've found history and science prove the Bible to be accurate, but we need to look at both the material and non-material worlds. The truth is, some facts are a smoke screen resulting from a lack of spiritual knowledge, which we can only receive by the counsel of the Holy Spirit, the Spirit of truth. In God's goodness, He gives us insight, knowledge and understanding into all things through the Spirit of truth. The opposite of God's goodness is pride, which produces evil.

Since creation, Satan has opposed God's goodness. I believe he does this because he once tasted the goodness of God. Now that he is not a part of it, he seeks revenge on God's beloved children. The creation of humanity is an expression of God's goodness. All of the good found in people is a reflection of God in them. Jesus made this clear:

Now as He was going out on the road, one came running, knelt before Him, and asked Him, "Good Teacher, what shall I do that I may inherit eternal life?" So, Jesus said to him, "Why do you call Me good? No one is good but One, that is, God" (Mark 10:17–18).

In this passage, a man ran up to Jesus, recognizing that He was good. Jesus then asked him a rhetorical question, not only proving that He is God, but also stating that only God is good. In other words, the man recognized Jesus as a good teacher, as a good man, but Jesus changed the perspective. He told him no one is good but God, implying that if He is good (which He is), then He is also God. Jesus and God are one (see John 10:30). If we are in Christ, we also have His goodness in us, but all the glory belongs to Him alone.

Although we who are saved have the goodness of God in us through Jesus, we still battle against the pride of our flesh. The only pride we should have is pride in God for His goodness and the way He allows us to share it with Him. Instead, angels, demons, and humans have been more proud of themselves than of the creator, which is the cause of evil in the world. However, the goodness of

God continues to turn what is meant for evil into something good (see Genesis 50:20). In the waiting, I have learned that God is good all the time. The kingdom of darkness (not God) is behind every evil device. Sometimes people find it easier to blame God instead of Satan. Some say, God could just stop Satan, but the truth is, He gave us power over the enemy, and we must exercise authority.

We can equate the fruit of goodness to something that tastes good. It's pleasant and fulfilling. As the psalmist wrote, *"Oh, taste and see that the Lord is good; Blessed is the man who trusts in Him" (Psalms 34:8).* The fruit of goodness brings light into darkness. The goodness of God is a safe spiritual shelter. When we are hidden in His goodness, no person or demon can snatch us from Him.

HE IS FAITHFUL

When I think of the fruit of faithfulness, I'm reminded that the fruit of the Spirit first belonged to the Holy Spirit. It's His divine nature flowing to and through us. Faithfulness has to do with trust, loyalty, deduction, steadfastness, and covenant commitment. Faithfulness is a force to be reckoned with, and it breaks through boundaries as strong as death. Before Jesus went to the cross, He asked God to take the cup of divine wrath away from Him, but because of faithfulness, He yielded to the will of the Father. We see His faithfulness in the way He prayed, *"Father, if You are willing, remove this cup [of divine wrath] from Me; yet not My will, but [always] Yours be done" (Luke 22:42 AMP).* His faithfulness in God's plan conquered death and brought forth eternal life.

When we think of the fruit of the Holy Spirit, we often think of ourselves, but let's focus on God for a moment. Consider how faithful the Holy Spirit is; He *never* leaves us. The Holy Spirit is even faithful to continually tug on the hearts of non-believers. Every night and day, the Holy Spirit seeks to give us counsel. He is our personal counselor, if we will listen. He seeks to teach us the word, if we will read it. He seeks to give us direction, if we will take it. He seeks to comfort us in times of grief, if we will accept it. He seeks to make a way where there is no way, if we will take a step of faith. The Holy Spirit is trustworthy, loyal to the core, steadfast, unwavering, and committed to our destiny in Christ. I pray the fruit of His faithfulness fills us so we can be faithful to God as well and then carry His faithfulness into the world. We will not make it out of the waiting until we have learned to be faithful.

A TOUCH OF GENTLENESS

God is a gentleman. Gentleness is a healing force. God's gentleness heals broken hearts, relationships, and marriages, and it bonds things together. As the psalmist wrote, *"You have also given me the shield of Your salvation; Your right hand has held me up, Your gentleness has made me great"(Psalms 18:35).* When we mess up and repent, God restores us through gentleness.

He always knocks on the doors of human hearts and comes in to meet with those who welcome Him. Satan, on the other hand, tries to force himself into people's lives. When I got pregnant out of wedlock, I felt defeated, guilty, and shameful. I felt like the devil lived rent-free in my head, whispering his lies in my mind. However, the gentleness of the Holy Spirit came in and gave me strength and hope as He ministered correction through love.

WALKING IN SELF-CONTROL

I imagine we all have a fruit of the Holy Spirit that is harder to walk in than others. For me, self-control has been hard. Yielding to the Holy Spirit in self-control takes great trust. If I freely yield to the Holy Spirit, I give Him control over myself. This is what Jesus did. He willingly gave up His will to follow the Father's will.

Self-control consists of self-discipline, which is hard for many people, but it is necessary for fulfilling our assignments and tasks. Whether people are believers or not, they feel a drive to complete tasks, no matter how small or great. It's part of how we're wired as humans. When people are born again, their spirits now feel driven to serve God; it's not forced, but becomes a natural force within. Yes, hindrances do sometimes get in the way of our personal and spiritual drive, usually requiring ministerial help. Yet even the choice to get help takes self-control. To stay in step with the Spirit, we must yield to the Holy Spirit who gives us self-control as He drives our will. Paul explained it this way:

I say then: Walk in the Spirit, and you shall not fulfill the lust of the flesh. For the flesh lusts against the Spirit, and the Spirit against the flesh; and these are contrary to one another, so that you do not do the things that you wish. But if you are led by the Spirit, you are not under the law. Now the works of the flesh are evident, which are: adultery, fornication, uncleanness, lewdness, idolatry, sorcery, hatred, contentions, jealousies, outbursts of wrath, selfish ambitions, dissensions, heresies, envy, murders, drunkenness, revelries, and the like; of which I tell you beforehand, just as I also told you in time past, that those who practice such things will not inherit the kingdom of God (Galatians 5:16–2)

The waiting process helped me develop the fruit of self-discipline in such a way that some people from my past hardly recognize me now. He will do the same for you.

MY TRIAL WITH JEZEBEL

Everyone who takes Christ seriously, especially those in ministry, will face the spirit of Jezebel many times. My battle with it was long and bumpy. I had seen the Jezebel spirit tear other churches apart, but this time it was right up in my business. Through the trial, I became so accustomed to the presence of witchcraft that I can now identify it quickly. I cannot say much about this particular event, but it was filled with empty words and broken promises. I learned that sometimes only God has your back. Thankfully, He did remove this spirit divinely. When people failed me, my God came through. I became very close to God in that season of my life. I learned a lot about spiritual warfare, and I received a greater measure of boldness. I discovered why, in Revelation 2:18–29, Jesus warned the church of Thyatira not to tolerate Jezebel. Jezebel isn't to be enabled, reasoned with, or coddled; this spirit must be confronted and thrown out.

People who are being controlled by the spirit of Jezebel will be compelled to act out in the following ways:

1. They will want to be in leadership or get close to leadership.
2. They are friendly unless they don't get their way or are confronted.
3. They don't have sound doctrine, but bring in mixture.
4. They form a group under them that they can "teach."
5. They are full of pride.
6. They are offended when they don't get leadership positions (that they never earned). Because of this, they church hop over and over.
7. They manipulate.
8. They usually have many deep wounds.
9. They usually reject the inner healing and deliverance process.
10. They are sexually deviant, although sometimes this is hidden. They may not display it publicly, but they struggle with porn, lust, and adultery behind the scenes.

TRIALS WITH BEING MISUNDERSTOOD

In the waiting, we are often misunderstood and discounted by many, both believers and non-believers. When this comes from those within the body of Christ, it has a different kind of blow. Unfortunately, if we're serious about the call of God on our lives, we will inevitably be told to quit by others. This is a sure sign to press in even harder. History shows us that pioneers are often misunderstood. Pioneers go into the land and take territory (physically and spiritually) while tearing down old, dead religious structures. When what was once dead and dry comes back to life, revival spontaneously breaks out.

The Spirit of God is powerfully at work, and I believe the next great awakening is upon us. This movement will surpass all previous moves because it will be larger and more widespread. In our culture, we can either be "woke" or awakened. During the Jesus Revolution in the 1970s, people were searching for love, and the demonic driving force behind it was a spirit of rebellion. As light clashed with darkness, God won; God is love. As people entered the Jesus Revolution movement, what had begun as a rebellion against parents, the government, and the dead religious system of the day, turned into a rebellion against the kingdom of darkness. During that time, some who were stuck in dead religion were wholly revived, while others stayed stuck in pride and tried to stop the movement. Regardless, God poured out His Spirit in great measure.

Let me give you a glimpse of what the Lord has shown me about this next movement. The Bible says we know in part and prophesy in part. So, I have a few pieces of the prophetic puzzle, and others will connect the rest. The 1970s saw a mass rebellion and a search for love. Today, we see mass witchcraft and a search for identity. Many people wonder who they are, what their pronouns are, and so forth. The spirit of witchcraft drives this; however, we will see the same response as we did during the Jesus Revolution.

I believe we will see a deliverance revolution because Satanism is in our faces at every corner. Blood is being splattered on many altars, while one drop of the blood of Jesus is sufficient to send every principality running. God is bringing deliverance—the casting out of demons—back into the body of Christ. Even the children will cast out demons in Jesus' name.

God has His hand on the millennials, Gen Z, and Gen Alpha. They will bring in the end-time harvest. The harvest is plentiful, but the laborers are few (see Matthew 9:37). People in the church have once again become stagnant and complacent, yet the next generation will take the lead. People say, "Revival isn't coming. The end times are here."

Why can't it be both? I believe it is both. As the world grows darker and the labor pains increase, God is birthing something in the midst of it all. The late prophet, Bob Jones, prophesied over twenty years ago that when the Kansas City Chiefs won the Super Bowl, a great revival movement would break out. Sports stadiums would be filled, and a billion people would come to know Christ. In 2023, the Grammys put on a satanic ritual performance on live television, the Chiefs won the Super Bowl, and a revival broke out at Asbury University among Gen Z and spread like wildfire. We see the puzzle coming together.

I was born for this. God has called to pioneer in this next movement. It will be a movement with many pioneers, not a one-person show. This movement will be worldwide, with many faces but one Spirit, many parts but one body. Many denominations will enter in, but the church will be of one mind. Of course, if you feel called to pioneer, know that people will let you down, misunderstand you, and try to veer you off track. That's OK. Pioneer anyway!

TRIALS FOR WOMEN IN MINISTRY

The idea that *"it's a man's world"* does not come from the mind of Christ. Genesis 1:27 says, *"God created man in His own image, in the image of God He created him; male and female He created them."* From the beginning, His vision included men and women working together in His image. Father God is often seen as a father in the natural—a warrior and a just judge, whereas the Holy Spirit is viewed in more feminine terms, comforting and helping. We see this picture in marriage when two become one. Male and female become one, just like both male and female are one in the image of God.

This book is not about proving women can work in ministry, although I know women are called to work in the five-fold offices spoken of in Ephesians. The early church functioned with both male and female leaders. The Bible speaks of Deborah, Esther, Phoebe, Junia, and Pricilla (and many others) who served in ministry leadership as women. For those who haven't studied ancient biblical history, lack knowledge of Hebrew and Greek terminology, and are unaware of women's roles in the early church, these two resources will be deeply helpful.

· *Women of Destiny* by Cindy Jacobs
· *Paulinian Church Order, The Women* by Dr. Ron Charles

Both books provide scriptural and historical evidence that can't be denied.

When Jesus rose from the dead, he first appeared to a woman, Mary Magdalene, who then spread the good news to the men. In the New Testament, women would prophesy in church. This implies they not only spoke in church, but spoke authoritatively, sharing the message of God with both men and women. Something is off in a person's interpretation if they believe women have no place in the church or can't talk in church. Taken at face value, this means a woman would sin by even saying "hello" to someone at church. Many women in the church don't cover their hair, yet if we take these verses at face value, that is also sin.

Imagine if the Samaritan woman at the well had preached the gospel to men (which she did) and they had said, *"No, I need a man to tell me."* Jesus could have chosen anyone, but He chose to reveal Himself as Messiah for the first time to a woman and to cultural outsiders. The Jews weren't supposed to speak to Samaritans, but Jesus chose a Samaritan woman to spread the gospel to Samaria. History tells us she was later martyred for preaching the gospel, and she continues to be held in great honor. It appears Jesus held women in higher esteem than some people do today, which should not be.

The scripture about having authority over a man is referring to marriage. Eve was created for Adam. Women are to honor and respect their husbands as the head of the home. And men are to love their wives as Christ did the church, being a servant and giving up His life out of love. When marriages work in this manner, the home is in order. However, in the church, we are one. Scripture clearly states there is no male or female in Christ, but we are all one (see Galatians 3:28). Male and female together complete the image of God (see Genesis 1:27).

Not all women stayed at home and cooked; that's a false

narrative. A woman's duty at home is certainly a priority, but some women have also led wars and served as great judges over men and women, such as Deborah. Some also worked the fields, while others led the churches with Paul.

Some people use Titus 1:6 as a disqualifier for women because it says an elder or overseer must be the husband of one wife. However, Titus 2 gives the qualifications of a godly woman.

Romans 16 lists Phoebe as a deacon:

I commend to you our sister Phoebe, a deacon of the church in Cenchreae. I ask you to receive her in the Lord in a way worthy of his people and to give her any help she may need from you, for she has been the benefactor of many people, including me. Greet Priscilla and Aquila, my co-workers in Christ Jesus. They risked their lives for me. Not only I but all the churches of the Gentiles are grateful to them. Greet also the church that meets at their house. Greet my dear friend Epenetus, who was the first convert to Christ in the province of Asia. Greet Mary, who worked very hard for you. Greet Andronicus and Junia, my fellow Jews who have been in prison with me. They are outstanding among the apostles, and they were in Christ before I was (Romans 16:1–7 NIV).

According to scholarly notes in the NIV, the word deacon in Romans 16:1 refers to a Christian designated to serve with the overseers or elders of the church in various ways (see also Phil 1:1; 1 Tim 3:8,12). The study of apologetics, eschatology, and hermeneutics is essential for those who desire to preach or teach the Bible.

I never planned to be a woman in ministry. I never aspired to do any of this when I was growing up. I had no real hope for a future and turned to education as an outlet. In the waiting season of my life, I earned an associates, bachelor's, and master's degree in three different fields, none of them were in biblical studies. All my schooling prepared me for the corporate world, but God had different plans and placed me as an agent in the spiritual world. So, if you're a woman who is called into five-fold ministry, be encouraged. Stand tall as the winds of opposition blow. You will be planted like a tree with deep roots if you humble yourself in the waiting.

POEM: DEAR BRIDE

Prepare, dear bride of Christ.
The lamps must be filled.
Await, for the calling is nigh.
Can you hear the thunder calling?
His voice stands firm.
The bell of liberty is ringing.

Arise, dear bride.
For the bridegroom awaits.
Look up, because our dear father calls your name.

Remnant, wake up and hear My voice.
My army is assembled.
We shall march on high.

The gathering has begun.
My saints are ready.
The battle has begun.

- Ruthie Dickey

11

FLIPPING TABLES

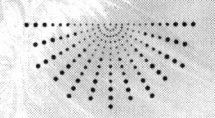

And Jesus entered the temple and drove out all those who were buying and selling in the temple, and overturned the tables of the money changers and the seats of those who were selling doves. And He said to them, "It is written, 'My house shall be called a house of prayer'; but you are making it a robbers' den." And the blind and the lame came to Him in the temple, and He healed them (Matthew 21:12–14 NASB1995).

One of the most important aspects of the waiting season is the process of personal holiness. God is calling us to holiness, both individually and corporately, but so many of us have become content chasing the American dream instead of God's dream.

HOW TO JUDGE PROPERLY

We need to awaken from our American dream and recognize the nightmare it has created in the church. The church isn't a building; it's a group of people called the body of Christ. We are the church.

The temple of God is found within us. We are a house for God, and we have become a sanctuary through consecration to the Lord. A sanctuary is a consecrated holy place of worship. To be holy is to be set apart. We are to be a peculiar people marked by His blood and nature. Instead, so many of us look like the world, act like the world, fit in with the world, and have the sulfur stench of demons.

Right now, two movements are taking place in our culture—the woke culture and the dreadful bride awakening. The dread champions are the bride of Christ who is "without spot or wrinkle" (Ephesians 5:27). The spot represents the stains of the world and the demonic kingdom of darkness, and the wrinkle represents the bending and folding to every cultural norm and doctrine of demons. The bride must be free of these things.

Jesus flipped tables in the temple because the judgment of God starts in the house of the Lord (see 1 Peter 4:17). God is dealing with our house first, and Jesus is about to flip some tables in our hearts that need to be overturned if we want seats at the wedding table of the Lamb. To have a seat at His table, we must let Him flip over ours. It's so easy for us all to point out the corruption in the church and world, but God always starts with the issues within each one of our hearts.

A time of judgment is here, and it's time for us to take our place as rightful judges in Christ. The Bible says that those who are spiritual will judge all things (see 1 Corinthians 2:15). We've all heard statements like, "We aren't to judge," or, "Who am I to judge?" but the Bible teaches us how to judge properly. *How* we judge matters greatly. We have a measuring stick to keep us in order.

The same measure we use to judge others, will be used to judge us. This is a good thing because it makes us evaluate ourselves first. Jesus tells us to remove the planks from our own eyes and then help our brother or sister in Christ remove the speck in their eyes. The end result should be two people coming out of sin and becoming consecrated together.

> *Do not judge so that you will not be judged. For in the way you judge, you will be judged; and by your standard of measure, it will be measured to you. Why do you look at the speck that is in your brother's eye, but do not notice the log that is in your own eye? Or how can you say to your brother, "Let me take the speck out of your eye," and behold, the log is in your own eye? You hypocrite, first take the log out of your own eye, and then you will see clearly to take the speck out of your brother's eye (Matthew 7:1–5 NASB1995).*

Jesus used the eye as a symbol here because we often judge by what we see in the natural or by what we see from our perspective, but we fail to see what's behind the curtain. This is why being filled with the Holy Spirit is so important. This is why the gift of discernment is vital. When we make judgments by what we see with the naked eye, those judgments can lead us astray. However, when the eyes of our heart are enlightened, we see with the eyes of the Father, making right judgments. The eyes of the Father reveal what's in a person's heart. Right judgment pierces the heart issues in someone's life.

We need to see from God's perspective, not our own, and when we judge, we should first ask the Lord to show us our own wickedness. When we deal with ourselves, the Lord will then use us to deal with the matters of others. The judgment of God ought to correct us before someone else has to. However, we all fail at times. Therefore, God set up His church to be a safe place of accountability. Some people say, *"I only answer to God, and I don't need any covering."* Yes, we do answer to God, but we also need to learn to recognize when God comes to us through a friend or trusted leader giving us correction. When we are close to God, we will recognize when He uses a familiar face to correct us. We see this throughout the Bible. We are accountable to godly counsel (see 1 Corinthians 5:12-13; 2 Samuel 12:1-7). In every situation, we should ask God to reveal where we may have pride and violently attack that pride through repentance, warfare, prayer, and fasting. Fasting is a great way to crush the serpent underfoot.

In the waiting, we are trained as royal priests and taught how to judge correctly. We can know we're growing into spiritual maturity when we can see our own shortcomings more than we can see the faults of others. We come to a place where we can confess our sins and be healed. We will have no issue apologizing to others and following it up with action. We must be a people of action, or our words are rubbish. During the waiting, God crushes all the footprints of pride in our lives. Pride leads to rebellion, and rebellion is as the sin of witchcraft (see 1 Samuel 15:23). Pride in life will eventually work as an open door for many demons to come in. Often, those who are proud don't know it because it's as if they are under a spell. I pray that any spell of deception is broken off you right now in Jesus' name.

When Jesus flips the tables of rebellion in our lives, He often does this by putting us under the leadership of a Saul personality type for a time. A Saul personality is an unpredictable leader, someone of many words who has to get the spotlight. Such leaders aren't likely to acknowledge us publicly and can get competitive when doors of opportunity open for us. Sometimes they will even try to steal our promotion. The Lord uses these situations and people, who often aren't even aware of their condition, to train us to submit and honor. It's difficult to respect, submit to, and honor those who operate under a Saul-type personality. However, doing this kills all pride within us, and God is more concerned with a humble heart than He is with opening doors. If our hearts are not humble, we will not have the character to sustain the doors that open before us in the future.

Keep in mind, *in the waiting*, we seem to encounter a push and shove at every corner. We experience significant resistance and many brick walls that need to be broken down. Every opportunity seems to come with a tug-of-war, and disappointment lurks around every corner. Hell seems to break loose at every prophetic word concerning our destiny. This happens because, in the waiting, we're being trained in the spiritual trenches to combat the kingdom of darkness while also learning to exercise our authority in Jesus Christ. When we eventually cross over from the waiting to the promised land, we won't experience so much striving. We won't face brick walls every step of the way. Instead, favor chases us down, and God opens doors no person can shut. Of course, we will also encounter giants that we have to overtake. The waiting prepares us to slay the giants in the promised land. That's why it's so important not to skip the waiting process, not to give up, and not to fold under pressure. Instead, we must meet with God in the secret place every day and, when we've done all, continue to stand.

The waiting season is typically years long, but we grow the most in this place. It's a place of preparation and consecration so that we can receive the restoration we need for the things ahead.

DEMONIC AGENDA IN THE AMERICAN CHURCH

In the American church, a demonic agenda of tolerance and lukewarmness has hovered over the body of Christ for so long. Still, God is raising up holy ones, dreadful ones, violent ones in the Spirit, who are yelling out like a voice in the wilderness, *"Prepare the way for the Lord, make straight paths for him" (John 1:23)*. In the waiting, our prayers are heard and echo forth throughout our wilderness season and manifest in the promised land. Remember that the waiting season has times of wandering in the wilderness, but it's not all wilderness. We will get little grassroots promotions, and how we handle them will determine how much more God entrusts to us.

I believe those who are in the waiting right now, and those who are coming out of the waiting right now, are the ones God has appointed specifically for this time to flip over the tables of the American church system. The American church has become a den of robbers—an enterprise and a place to make lots of money for self-gain. I am not against making lots of money. And I don't believe we have to be poor to be righteous. Many of the men and women of God in the Bible were blessed with financial wealth. Having wealth is not the issue, but the love of money becomes the root of all evil (see 1 Timothy 6:10). Our true riches are spiritual. God gives

His people money to further His kingdom, but our focus must be on God's kingdom, not on our bank accounts.

Before we can get promoted, we must get our heart motives right concerning money. When people take shortcuts in the waiting process, they often experience discord in their lives as they get intoxicated with influence and money—forgetting their first love. They become enamored with the praises of people, the crowds, and the social media status, and they neglect to be known by God. Sure, they will make God known by saying His name. That's how they got their fame, but it becomes prostitution of the kingdom. This will not be tolerated. It's better to be known by God than make Him known with a wrong motive. We can prophesy, cast out demons, and heal the sick, but if we neglect our relationship with God, we will hear the scariest words ever uttered by God, "Depart from me. I do not know you." Jesus made it clear:

Not everyone who says to Me, "Lord, Lord," will enter the kingdom of heaven, but he who does the will of My Father who is in heaven will enter. Many will say to Me on that day, "Lord, Lord, did we not prophesy in Your name, and in Your name cast out demons, and in Your name perform many miracles?" And then I will declare to them, "I never knew you; depart from Me, you who practice lawlessness" (Matthew 7:21–23 NASB1995).

Many men and women of God started out pure, with authentic anointing, but somewhere along the way a little fox came in and robbed the Holy Spirit of His spotlight. This is why so many churches in America have shut down. People have rejected the move of the Holy Spirit and injected their man-made agendas into the veins of the people. But the sheep have had enough. They are looking for their shepherd. Those who are called by God are the children of God; they are the sheep who hear the shepherd's voice. Unfortunately, the real voice of the Lord is not sounded in many churches, so people have left the building. The church as we know it is being reconstructed. This isn't something new or outside of scripture. It's going back to the original design, as we see in the book of Acts. Let the book of Acts church arise and the dead bones come alive.

As God moves corporately and suddenly onto the scene, the tables of influence will be flipped, the tables of the false prophets will be flipped, the table of perversion will be flipped, and the table of self-promotion will be flipped. Speaking of self-promotion, this is something the Lord spoke with me about many years ago. He told me through various means what was to come in my life. Many of these things have come to pass already, and some of these things are still in the works. One of the things He told me very clearly was to never promote myself but to let Him open the doors.

I'm not talking about advertising an event. I'm talking about squeezing my way into the green rooms of others or inviting myself into places. Self-promotion at its core comes whenever someone tries to bump shoulders with those who can give them influence. People who self-promote are internally terrified that someone might rise above them, so they sow seeds of discord and puff themselves up. The same people tell grandiose stories, promise others the world, tell them precisely what they want to hear, and prophesy extravagantly, but they genuinely don't care about people. In fact, these types of people only keep their word if it will benefit them. They have lost focus on their first love.

This is the opposite of leadership. Authentic leaders serve others and want to see them rise above, even if that means they surpass them. True leaders know when to pass the baton to the next generation. True leaders are not on social media every day, posting twenty videos begging for likes and shares, but they are in the quiet place seeking the Lord. They don't chase promotion; promotion chases them. When we enter into the promised land because of promotion from the Lord, the favor of God will chase us down. God's divine promotion takes us places only seen in our wildest dreams. This is exactly what He did with Joseph when He made Joseph's brothers and people from many nations bow down before him, but it came after fifteen-plus years of waiting, jealousy, accusations, and imprisonment.

Some people will push, pull, and shove their way in, trampling down someone else's door and stealing their promotion. I've had this happen in my own life. If this has happened to you, please take heart. The Lord doesn't need those people to make His plans happen in your life. He will open another door. When you are disappointed by an opportunity that suddenly closed, humble yourself, seek the Lord, and wait for Him to move again. When promotion suddenly slips out of your grip, rest assured that the Lord has a plan. His plan will be worth the wait.

We must not be enamored by people with a platform or social media stars who film all their own stuff. Some of this is good and ordained by God, but we must examine the fruit to know the authenticity of the spirit at work. We must also avoid being influenced by the disgruntled—those who have tried to gain people's attention but failed. They claim everyone is a "false prophet," especially those who have influence. They become heresy hunters, but in this season, they will be hunted themselves. When we curse others undeservingly, it comes back on us. We are called to bless people, not curse them. We can judge spiritual truths and doctrines, but we aren't called to set out to destroy others. Of course, if a false prophet, witch, or warlock really is in the church, we must call them out, sometimes by name. But we need to use wisdom and seek counsel before doing so.

In addition, we must avoid preachers who teach that certain gifts of the spirit have passed away and that apostles and prophets no longer exist. These same people still believe in pastors, evangelists, and teachers, but want to ignore the full meaning of Ephesians 4:11. The Lord is flipping the tables of dead religion that has words but no power.

But realize this, that in the last days, difficult times will come. For men will be lovers of self, lovers of money, boastful, arrogant, revilers, disobedient to parents, ungrateful, unholy, unloving, irreconcilable, malicious gossips, without self-control, brutal, haters of good, treacherous, reckless, conceited, lovers of pleasure rather than lovers of God, holding to a form of godliness, although they have denied its power; avoid such men as these. For among them are those who enter into households and captivate weak women weighed down with sins, led on by various impulses, always learning and never able to come to the knowledge of the truth. Just as Jannes and Jambres opposed Moses, so these men also oppose the truth, men of depraved mind, rejected in regard to the faith. But they will not make further progress; for their folly will be obvious to all, just as Jannes's and Jambres's folly was also (2 Timothy 3:1–9 NASB1995).

The real gospel is backed up by demonstration. Miracles are a reality. When we are full of the Holy Spirit, He manifests through us in signs and wonders.

This is especially important today because a revival of witchcraft is sweeping through the land. This is the counterfeit move and the great storm the world is facing. But the rivers of witchcraft will not overwhelm the flood of the Holy Spirit. As followers of Christ, we must take a stand against this agenda that is being pushed out specifically upon our children. Toy stores sell Ouija boards and witches cauldrons, and surprisingly, many Christians think it's cute. Witchcraft will destroy a person's life from the inside out. Witchcraft is real and has great power, even the ability to kill. People die at the hands of demons daily, unaware of the spiritual darkness that has been lurking under their noses for many years. All sorts of mental illnesses and physical sicknesses come upon people when they open doors to demons. Witchcraft is one of those doors.

One example of this is the celebration of Halloween. This is the second most holy day for Satanists. Halloween is a sacred day for them to worship their god. God started pressing me about this issue many years ago, and as I studied it, I couldn't deny that Halloween is evil. Watching Halloween movies that glamorize demons, witches, and murder is spiritual adultery to God. When I stepped away from this holiday, repented, canceled the curses, and shut this door in my life, my life changed for the better. My children don't have nightmares, mental oppression, or strange illnesses, and it's because we work diligently to keep doors to the demonic shut. When they are older, the choice will be theirs, but as a parent, I will stand before God and give an account for how I raised them. Witchcraft of any kind is forbidden in scripture, and it brings a curse upon a person's life. If you think it's hard to abstain from one truly evil holiday once a year, you might still have some spots and wrinkles you need to address. This is a day and time when the Lord is flipping over the tables of witchcraft.

We've entered a new era in which the very fabric of the church is being unwoven. The old ways of doing things here in America are passing away so that new wine can be poured into new a wineskin. The Lord has raised up a generation that is getting ready to march to the forefront. Some of these people are still in the waiting, while others are already pioneering heavily. The pioneers have been pushed to the side, rejected, and neglected, but they are coming out of the cave with the fiery flame of God in their eyes. They have nothing to lose and everything to gain. We will see a rise of sacred meetings with these pioneers. These pioneers will host the presence of God, which is contrary to what has been seen for many years. They understand that upper room experiences don't need a camera, because some meetings are too sacred to share. They will be known for hosting meetings where you just have to be there to see it.

Also, many of the forerunners in the body of Christ are not American (although, many do still exist here in the U.S. as well). These forerunners are found in the underground churches in other countries, and they are living under a type of persecution not yet seen here in the U.S. These people literally live out the gospel, and their children raise the dead. Many of us are only accustomed to the westernized church in America, and we fail to realize our brothers and sisters in other nations are dying for their faith. They go out at night to minister to the one lost soul. They hold underground revivals knowing they may get shot up at any moment. Many women and young girls are even raped for being Christians. The horrors they face are terrifying, but their faith is electrifying. Many books, documentaries, television shows, podcasts, and testimonies speak about these amazing people of God. Researching the persecuted church across the world, gives us a window into faith and power at a level that is rare in the U.S.

These people are genuinely spreading the raw, authentic gospel of Jesus with no public reward, payment, or fame except the reward they get from God. We often hear it preached in America that if we pray in private then God will reward us publicly. We tend to think this means God will allow others to see how great we are, but what if the reward is also about the day of judgment when those who followed Christ will hear "well done my good and faithful servant"? This is the reward we should want—instead of fame before people. This is why Jesus warned His disciples:

Beware of practicing your righteousness before other people in order to be seen by them, for then you will have no reward from your Father who is in heaven. Thus, when you give to the needy, sound no trumpet before you, as the hypocrites do in the synagogues and in the streets, that they may be praised by others. Truly, I say to you, they have received their reward. But when you give to the needy, do not let your left hand know what your right hand is doing, so that your giving may be in secret. And your Father who sees in secret will reward you. And when you pray, you must not be like the hypocrites. For they love to stand and pray in the synagogues and at the street corners, that they may be seen by others. Truly, I say to you, they have received their reward. But when you pray, go into your room and shut the door and pray to your Father who is in secret. And your Father who sees in secret will reward you (Matthew 6:1–6 ESV).

The Lord has given me several words about this over the past few years, which I share below. I hope these words encourage you. I believe Jesus is flipping the tables of the current corruption in the church, and He is setting a new table before the remnant, and these prophetic words speak to that.

A TIME OF MULTIPLICATION! THE UNDERDOG ARISE. (JULY 2022)

A time is coming soon when you will see the rise of men and women of God who aren't concerned with titles or affirmation. They know who they are in Christ, and that's the only affirmation they need. You will see an increase of the word of God being preached with power and demonstration. You will see streams of deliverance, prophecy, and healing taking place all at once. These people will be wholly yielded to the Holy Spirit, and all nine gifts will manifest through their yielded vessels of dust.

You will see many who aren't famous coming out of the woods, so to speak, and they will have a focus like that of Smith Wigglesworth. Wigglesworth was a man who believed every word in the Bible, sometimes too literally. He was obedient to the voice of God and would travel far to minister to just one low-class person. He would also walk up to dead bodies and say, "Rise up in Jesus' name," and they would come back to life. He was trained as a plumber in the natural but trained by the Holy Spirit in everything else. These ones are coming forth.

Watch as "revival hubs" spring up in homes and churches. These will be places where cameras don't go. They will be sacred meetings where the only speaker is the Holy Spirit. These will be known as revelation encounters, and the word of God will back them up. People will say, "Oh, this is what the scripture was talking about all along."

WATCH AND SEE. (AUGUST 18, 2021)

I believe the Lord is saying He is still cleaning house. Churches will empty out. Large churches will also empty (*because of resisting the Holy Spirit*), and the remnant book-of-Acts church will arise. The Lord is building up a mighty and dreadful people—His dread champions. Watch as churches are emptied (after I got this word, the second largest church in my town closed, as well as a few others).

God is equipping people to take authority over demons because demonic powers are increasing. This is not something new or unheard of but is the same warfare we see in scripture. We are in the last days, and the enemy is trying to speed things up. But the Lord Almighty has the last word, and He sits on His throne and laughs. Satan will be made to work for Him, and all his plans will fail exactly how God has planned.

This is a season of the testing of our faith and dedication to the Lord. Whose side are you on? Who is number one? Who will you believe? "Be at perfect peace," says the Lord. "I hold death and life in My hands, and there is no death in Christ Jesus."

Vision: I see someone prophesying the word of the Lord and rushing fire coming out of their mouth. Some people's anointing comes out of their mouths by the breath of God. The word of God is powerful, active, and alive, sharper than any two-edged sword. The word of the Lord will never fail.

The Lord says, "Stand up, oh saints. Kneel to Me, and I will show you what must take place. Stop looking in the natural, for it's not as it seems. I am sending a mighty force of angels, and you will see the manifestation of this spiritual war in the natural. Get your strategies in the secret place, the place where you are seated with Christ. It's your job to manifest heaven on earth. You are hidden in Christ, and Christ is in you, the hope of glory. You have everything you need. Jesus is the word. You have all you need. So, take up the full armor of God and march forward. You have nothing to fear. Encourage one another and carry their burdens, lifting them up."

"Don't be alarmed at wars and rumors of wars, for I said this would be so." A showdown is about to happen, and what might feel like complete chaos for a time is actually bringing forth divine order by God.

ROSH HASHANAH (SEPTEMBER 19, 2022)

Rosh Hashanah 5783 starts on September 25—the Jewish New Year. Here is what I hear the Lord saying.

"Watch as I do a work among the people so mighty that the awe and fear of who I am will move across the world."

"Look among the nations! Observe! Be astonished! Wonder! Because I am doing something in your days—You would not believe it if you were told" (see Habakkuk 1:5).

"Africa will see Me, and I will tear down their witchcraft with holy violence. Asia will see My outpouring, and missionaries will be sent forth. I will start to restore the land of Australia, and My song will go forth. North America, I'm coming for you. America, you have become like Israel in the book of Ezekiel, but My prophets shall speak and warn of what's to come. I'm awakening my people in America, and I will move in mighty power through those who will humble themselves and serve others. You shall see a face of Me not seen since Moses on Mount Sinai" (see Exodus 34:29–35).

This is a time when the Lord is reconstructing the church. We will see the emptying of places of worship and the removal of people who refuse to allow the Spirit of God to move freely. We will see many churches rise up. Some will be in buildings and others in houses. These places will be houses/churches of prayer; they will meet with the Lord and get strategies to advance His kingdom. I hear God saying, "I'm restoring prayer to My church." These will be places for authentic discipleship. However, the church is a people, and His people will take the "church" to the world. I see church services being held in hair salons, malls, grocery stores, shopping centers, corn fields, bars, coffee shops, schools, and gyms. The people of God will be sent out into the world. It's time. It's time.

It's time to get serious for God. There is a grace right now to choose God. There is a grace to get your house in order. There is a grace to reconcile and forgive. There is a grace to move into the old mantles you left on the floor. Choose who you will serve. You can't serve God and Baal. Hear the Spirit of the Lord.

Ezekiel's book will parallel this day and time (5783) from 2023 to 2025. You will see dry bones come alive and resurrection power restored to His people. As witchcraft rises, so does God's authority in His people. Witchcraft has power, but the Spirit of God has authority, which trumps power. It's time now to shut all doors to the enemy. Stop giving the devil a place. Protect the children, for we will give an account for what we allowed to come over our children.

Humble yourself today under the mighty shadow of the Lord and you will be exalted. You will walk through the valley of the shadow of death, but you will not be harmed. Arise, oh violent ones, and take the kingdom by force (see Matthew 11:12).

Just as He did for the prophet Isaiah, the Lord is cleaning the mouth (as we are in the decade of the mouth) with His coals.

POEM: HIS SWEETNESS

May the sweet sounds of the Lord fill my ears. May His glory shine upon my face. His glory is at hand. His sounds ring clear. The birds sing His name. They shout it on high. The moon shines upon His creation.

Lord, I bless Your mighty name.
Lord, I praise You with my song.
You are worthy to be exalted.
My lips say Your name with wonder.

I sing a song of gladness.
My heart leaps with joy.
Forever praises are in my mind.
I speak of Your love forever.
The universe calls His name.

-Ruthie Dickey

12

FRIEND OF GOD

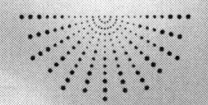

The most important part of the waiting is developing friendship with God. It is the foundation of our faith and everything else we are called to do. There is a difference between being called and chosen. In the first chapter, I talked about being called by God, which is an invitation. Being chosen by God is saying yes in surrender to Him and is not something to take lightly. The calling of the Lord comes with a choice. However, when we choose Him, it's because He first chose us and called us out of the darkness and into the light. He is the light in the darkness. It's a heavy, weighty glory to be chosen. It's supernatural—a divine destiny written before the ages. As we enter into real friendship with Jesus, we walk into our destiny.

THE GIFTS OF THE SPIRIT CONCERNING THE BODY OF CHRIST

Along the way, we will find other Christian friends, some who stay and some who go. Some will take our hand and guide us to new heights with the Lord. These are the ones who love us enough to correct us. The ones who come and go are the ones we don't need for the long haul, but they are beneficial for a time. Pray blessings over them and release them. We are all one body with many parts, and we need each other. As Paul wrote:

Now, there are varieties of gifts, but the same Spirit. And there are varieties of ministries, and the same Lord. There are varieties of effects, but the same God who works all things in all persons. But to each one is given the manifestation of the Spirit for the common good. For to one is given the word of wisdom through the Spirit, and to another the word of knowledge according to the same Spirit; to another faith by the same Spirit, and to another gifts of healing by the one Spirit, and to another the effecting of miracles, and to another prophecy, and to another the distinguishing of spirits, to another various kinds of tongues, and to another the interpretation of tongues. But one and the same Spirit works all these things, distributing to each one individually just as He wills. For even as the body is one and yet has many members, and all the members of the body, though they are many, are one body, so also is Christ. For by one Spirit we were all baptized into one body, whether Jews or Greeks, whether slaves or free, and we were all made to drink of one Spirit. For the body is not one member, but many. If the foot says, "Because I am not a hand, I am not a part of the body," it is not for this reason any the less a part of the body. And if the ear says, "Because I am not an eye, I am not a part of the body," it is not for this reason any the less a part of the body. If the whole body were an eye, where would the hearing be? If the whole were hearing, where would the sense of smell be? But now God has placed the members, each one of them, in the body, just as He desired. If they were all one member, where would the body be? But now there are many members, but one body. And the eye cannot say to the hand, "I have no need of you"; or again the head to the feet, "I have no need of you." On the contrary, it is much truer that the members of the body which seem to be weaker are necessary; and those members of the body which we deem less honorable, on these we bestow more abundant honor, and our less presentable members become much more presentable (1 Corinthians 12:4–23 NASB1995).

These verses tell us there is one Spirit but many gifts. We understand the gifts come from the precious Spirit of truth, the Holy Spirit. He desires to be our best friend so that He can manifest through us. He does that through the spiritual gifts He gives us. In fact, He wants each of us in the body of Christ to walk in the gifts of the Spirit. It's interesting to see the gifts of the Spirit and the functionality of the body of Christ grouped together. This shows us for the body to be whole all members need to operate in their gifting. On the other end of the spectrum, demonic spirits also need a body to manifest through to cause the most damage. Sure, they can move things around in homes and make noises and shadows in the night, but to be effective, they want to be inside a person and compel that person to act out Satan's will. By contrast, the Holy Spirit manifests through us to do God's will. The devil tries to counterfeit everything that God does. He wants to be greater than God because he's filled with pride and fear. When we see pride or fear, we can know we're in the arena of the devil. We saw this scenario with the magicians of Egypt and Moses.

Then Pharaoh also called for the wise men and the sorcerers, and they also, the magicians of Egypt, did the same with their secret arts. For each one threw down his staff, and they turned into serpents. But Aaron's staff swallowed up their staffs (Exodus 7:11–12 NASB1995).

God's authority burst forth as Aaron's staff swallowed up the enemy's power. I have learned through deliverance ministry that witchcraft has great power but lacks authority. The blood of Jesus is our authority.

In the body of Christ, we all need each other. We make up a body, like a team or a family. We all have different assignments and functions. What we need is unity. If we are fully yielded to the Holy Spirit, He can manifest more than one of His gifts through us, just as He did with the disciples. Many of us will operate in one main gift most of the time, but we will still operate in others at various times. For example, some people operate in the gift of healing every time they pray, but they only prophesy occasionally. One person may work miracles but lack the interpretation of tongues. Nonetheless, we need the interpretation of tongues.

My ministry team and partners come together relying on each other's gifts during revival meetings. We aren't in competition but instead lean into each other's strengths and gifting. At times, one of us has smelled the fragrance of heaven, while another has received a prophetic word, and another has received a word of knowledge. Working together like this has caused an electric unity that has bolted through the atmosphere. One recent example of this happened at the Soar Texas Women's Event in 2022. As the Soar team prayed over a lady, each of our gifts manifested corporately through words of knowledge, prophecy, and distinguishing of spirits. The word of knowledge gave her the faith to receive, the prophetic word gave her hope for the future, and the distinguishing of spirits manifested through a sweet smell, letting us all know the Lord was present. As a result, heaven manifested on earth in a tangible way, and she was filled with the Holy Spirit and delivered from demons.

Truly, we must learn to rely on each other. I've witnessed such a lack of honor in the body of Christ, especially in the waiting season. This lack of honor results from a competitive spirit. People who want to be competitive should join sports teams, not enter the ministry.

Rather than competing with one another, we must honor one another and be careful to not think so highly of ourselves. We honor God by how we honor each other. This includes how we treat our spouses. If your marriage is a mess, get it in order. Marriage isn't about your happiness; it's a training ground where you learn to be a holy servant, putting your needs last. How we treat lowly people in society is also a glimpse into our relationship with God. In the waiting, we learn to be friends of God by being good friends to others. Our friendship with others is a reflection of our friendship with God.

When we rid ourselves of competition in the body of Christ, then we can be a unit working as one. When we compete with each other, we look like a track athlete trying to run with one leg but walking with the other. Even the disciples failed in this area at times. As Jesus told them He was about to die, the disciples argued about *who among them was greatest*. We ought to learn from their mistakes, not repeat them.

When the hour had come, He reclined at the table, and the apostles with Him. And He said to them, "I have earnestly desired to eat this Passover with you before I suffer; for I say to you, I shall never again eat it until it is fulfilled in the kingdom of God." And when He had taken a cup and given thanks, He said, "Take this and share it among yourselves; for I say to you, I will not drink of the fruit of the vine from now on until the kingdom of God comes." And when He had taken some bread and given thanks, He broke it and gave it to them, saying, "This is My body which is given for you; do this in remembrance of Me." And in the same way He took the cup after they had eaten, saying, "This cup which is poured out for you is the new covenant in My blood. But behold, the hand of the one betraying Me is with Mine on the table. For indeed, the Son of Man is going as it has been determined; but woe to that man by whom He is betrayed!" And they began to discuss among themselves which one of them it might be who was going to do this thing. And there arose also a dispute among them as to which one of them was regarded to be greatest. ...[But Jesus said,] "But it is not this way with you, but the one who is the greatest among you must become like the youngest, and the leader like the servant. For who is greater, the one who reclines at the table or the one who serves? Is it not the one who reclines at the table? But I am among you as the one who serves" (Luke 22:14–24, 26–27 NASB1995).

The disciples were in one of the most profound spiritual moments of their lives as Jesus told them what was to come. In that holiest of moments, as Jesus prophesied the future, the presence of the Lord must have been overwhelming in that place. Yet, the disciples still managed to get distracted by focusing on themselves. Many of us have been guilty of this before. Although we are in a meeting where the presence of God is so thick, we feel the need to prove our worth to someone else. The first step to overcoming this problem is recognizing it and then getting deliverance from the spirit of competition. This is so important because competition kills our relationship with the Holy Spirit. It grieves Him.

THE CLOSER WE GET, THE SMALLER WE BECOME

When the Lord uses us in miraculous ways and we become mature Christians, the result should be a diminishing of our ego. The greater the working of the Holy Spirit through us, the smaller we should feel, not vice versa. True lovers of God are humbled by the evidence of God's work through their lives, because they know they can do nothing aside from Him. In the waiting, others are promoted all around us, and it's our job to cheer them on. We should jump for joy when someone else is lifted high. In my waiting season, I watched others rise to new heights, and I looked at it as an opportunity to learn from them, to sit under them, and to serve. In the waiting, we will serve without pay for years. The waiting period is a training for the promised land. Then when we walk into the promised land, others will come alongside us to serve us on our Christ-given missions. At that point, we will most likely start receiving payment and become sought after in whatever sector the Lord has placed us. For some, it's the five-fold ministry; for others, it's business, politics, education, media, family, or the arts. No matter what mountain of influence we are called to, if we skip over the process in the waiting season, our character will be lacking, and pride will be our fall. The waiting season is one of the most beautiful seasons of life. I look at it like a classroom. In fact, in the waiting season, I often dreamed about being in a classroom, which symbolized I was being trained and tested.

In the waiting, as we yield to God, all people pleasing, need for approval from others, and insecurity will be crushed and swept into the trash. This process, in the end, is a fresh wind of relief. We leave it knowing nothing can hold us back anymore. We learn to be okay with not always being liked and with being misunderstood. In the waiting, we discover we have nothing to lose and all of heaven is cheering us on.

However, the waiting is also a place of much heartache and many tears. God meets us in that place with His healing power. The heartache will be healed, and every deep wound will be exposed and dealt with. God takes our hearts of stone and gives us new hearts, hearts of gold, hearts that are after God. We are renewed, and the old is removed. Though it's painful, this process is so deeply important. We must not give in to the temptation to skip it.

A FRIEND THAT STICKS CLOSER THAN A BROTHER

In the waiting, friendships often shift. As I talked about previously, we often experience betrayal, which trains us in forgiveness and holiness. The betrayals often are a part of God's plan, but even if they aren't, He makes everything work together for good for those who love Him. The Bible says God sends an angel to separate the wheat from the tares within the body of Christ (see Matthew 13:24-30). He does the same thing in our lives as He separates our friends, the wheat from the tares. He plucks out the people-pleasers, the users, the abusers, the gossipers, the liars, and every other so-called friend who isn't there to produce the harvest in our lives.

God is actually giving us royal families as He cleans up our friend lists. As it says in Proverbs, *"A man of too many friends comes to ruin, but there is a friend who sticks closer than a brother" (Proverbs 18:24 NASB1995).* Some people will be in our lives for a season and for a specific purpose that comes to ruin later. These friendships don't last and usually cause pain, but the pain is worth all that we gain. Let me illustrate with a few of my own experiences.

But first, let me clarify. If you are not being a good friend to others—if you gossip, are self-centered, and have friendships only when it benefits you—when people walk away from you, God was not removing friends from your life. Instead, your actions caused natural consequences. We all fail in friendships, so if this is you, don't be so hard on yourself. But do change. We want to be a blessing to others, not a curse. We do not want to be the ones who cause others to learn the hard friendship lessons. At one time in my life, I was all of the things I listed above. I was a curse, not a blessing, and I was the one who caused pain. Once I realized this, I corrected it.

I'm a very loyal, loving, and giving person. Unfortunately, I have often been let down by others who have not been that way in return. This was also naive of me, to expect others to reciprocate. We ought to give without expecting anything in return, yet staying in one-sided friendships is unwise. We cannot blame everything that happens in friendships on somebody else. We must first take the plank out of our own eye, and then we will see clearly how to remove it from others.

At one time, I had a group of friends around me that God told me to let go. At the time, I didn't fully understand what was happening. Because of the abandonment in my past, I struggled to let anyone go. But I did it, and it was the best decision I ever made. Quickly, it became very clear I had been unequally yoked with people who claimed Christ but didn't live it out. If I hadn't walked away, I would have continued down the same path as them. When I chose to be obedient to God in this area of my life, He immediately gave me strength to press forward. God was separating me for a purpose; it wasn't so much about them, but about His desire to help me become all He created me to be. The loneliness of losing these friends swiftly faded, and I felt more company in my relationship with God than in my friendships in the world.

HE NEEDS US ALL TO HIMSELF

In the waiting, through the trials concerning friendships, I learned I was like a puppet, and too many people were pulling my strings. God detached me from those unfruitful relationships in order to prune me so I could later produce much fruit. The Lord took me into His love chamber, which I call the secret place of the Most High. He taught me how to have a relationship with Him, how to be comfortable in a room sitting alone for hours in His presence, and what it meant to be the bride of Christ. He did this by strengthening my relationship with my husband.

My marriage was a big mess that I thought needed to be burned in the fire, but instead, God took us to the refiner's fire, where He purified us. This took years, but I never lost faith, because I saw my husband slowly changing as he listened to God's voice. It was a very rough time, with lots of backtracking, but also lots of hope. If you're in this place, do not give up. Of course, you can't force your spouse to follow God. Many women have been counseled in the wrong way. They have been told that if they only pray harder and have more faith, their husband will straighten up. I disagree. In prayer, we cannot violate someone's free will. That is witchcraft. In addition, prayer is not about getting our way (as we covered in the previous chapters), but about aligning with God's will and having faith regardless of our circumstances.

When we pray for our spouses, the Holy Spirit and His angels, who are called His ministering spirits, are sent forth to whisper in their ears and draw them toward God's will, but it's still up to them to choose. Prayer does make a huge difference in the lives of others, but most of all, prayer makes a difference in our own lives. When people fail us, God's love propels us into our destiny. I am glad that my husband chose to follow God. That is our unique testimony. If the relationship you long for hasn't worked out, or the marriage you prayed for has shattered into a million pieces, know this: The Lord will gather up every broken piece and paint a new picture in your life.

FROM SEARCHING TO RESTING

At the beginning of life, we are all searching. Some of us have found what we were searching for and can now rest. All we long for is answered in the person of the Holy Spirit. The Holy Spirit is not an it, but a person, a part of the Godhead, and He is always with those who receive Him. The Holy Spirit will even minister to those who do not believe. He will show Himself to those who despise Him. He never gives up on us because He is the essence of love. God loved us so much that he gave us His only begotten Son. However, He didn't just give us Jesus, the Son of God, God in the flesh. He also gave us His Spirit, the Spirit of Truth, who is holy and set apart and made to fit inside of us like a puzzle piece.

As you yield to Him, a sweet relationship will arise, and the missing pieces of your life will come together. You will soon realize everything's about Him. Outside of Him, life is meaningless. We need to look at the Holy Spirit for who He is, a person with feelings. It is possible to grieve the Holy Spirit, and we must be careful not to do so. We can also please the Holy Spirit with our faith and by choosing to spend time with Him. The Holy Spirit wants to talk to us even more than we want to listen. He loves to speak, and He loves when we love on Him.

Throughout the waiting season, I have learned to love on the Holy Spirit like my best friend. In fact, the Holy Spirit is closer to me than anyone else. It only makes sense that I should pour my affection out on Him. In the middle of the night, when I call on the name of the Lord, the Holy Spirit is with me. Whenever I cry over the hardships of parenting, the Holy Spirit guides me. Whenever I am overwhelmed by marriage, the Holy Spirit advises me and counsels me. Whenever I want to give up on ministry, the Holy Spirit reminds me who it's all about and why I must finish my race. Whenever I am upset and think I'm all alone, the Holy Spirit waits for me. The Holy Spirit always answers the call whenever I speak to Him. The Holy Spirit never rejects, abandons, betrays, or denies me. The Holy Spirit is always with me.

The Holy Spirit is also with you, and He wants a relationship with you. You can stop searching. What you long for—His presence, His peace, and His power to change every circumstance—is already with you.

SPIRIT-TO-SPIRIT COMBAT

We live in a spiritual battle, and if we want to combat the enemy, we must get spiritual. If God removed the veils from our eyes, we would see that everything in the natural is a byproduct of the supernatural.

The unseen realm created the physical realm. The unseen realm affects everything in the physical realm. Principalities, powers, and rulers of darkness in the heavens battle against the angels of the Lord. Warfare rages in the heavens and on earth. In some people, the Spirit of God manifests, and in others, the spirit of the devil manifests. Most people are so accustomed to their flesh that they deny their human spirit. This is scary because those who are unaware of their triune being, can be easily used for evil. Evil spirits see people's bodies as houses they can occupy. We must be so careful and sensitive to the Holy Spirit that we only allow Him to manifest in and through us.

A FRIEND OF GOD

Some of you who read this may just be entering into the waiting, and I hope you are inspired by what you've read. Be expectant and excited about what the Lord will do in your life. Embrace the refiner's fire and let His launders soap purify you. We all aspire for the better in our lives, but the better only comes from *the waiting*. In the waiting, we are not just waiting on God, but He is also waiting on us. We must trust Him in the waiting room. In the waiting room, we feel so much anticipation for what is to come. It's a place of excitement and expectancy; our hearts' expectancy produces the currency of faith needed to see the next door open.

If you're in the middle of the waiting season, don't give up. You've made it this far, and God has so much more for you. Take one day at a time, take a deep breath, and reminisce on all the things that have already happened. Remember, waiting is not supposed to be passive, but active. It's a day-by-day journey with God that involves discipline, obedience, and renewing the mind, which all require acting on something. You're not waiting passively to get to the promised land; you're acting aggressively to push down every hinderance that separates you from God.

I believe some of you reading this book have been in the waiting and have grown weary. This is because your mind is negative and requires renewing. You must renew your mind daily, which happens through reading God's word. Choose today to read the word and believe the word. Do not believe what you see or what you hear in the natural but believe the word of God. Renew your mind and watch as things change. Some of you have hindered your waiting season by neglecting the truth and believing lies. Truth and lies are on the balance beam. I hope you decide to tip it toward the truth, but the choice is yours. Some of you are about to come out of the waiting season very soon, feeling as if you're in labor and about to give birth, and it's because you are. So keep pushing.

If you have come out of the waiting season and entered your promised land, you may in the future find yourself in another waiting room with the Lord, and if you do, I hope you will remember the words of this book.

Initially, this book had only nine chapters. When I was on the last chapter, the Lord changed my plans through a dream at night. In the dream, I was with an old friend, and we were discussing the last details before publishing this book. All of a sudden, I saw the book chapters written out, and to my surprise there was twelve, but I couldn't make out what the titles of the remaining chapters were. In addition, I knew the last chapter would be a song title, this was made clear in the dream. I wrote this dream down in my journal and continued writing this book for many months. Turns out, I needed more chapters because I still needed to finish living them out. For three months, I lived out each chapter. The Lord gave me the titles to the remaining three chapters through a word of knowledge, but none of them was a song title, so I felt perplexed.

I thought maybe the dream was more symbolic than literal, as dreams usually are. During those few months, I had found myself in the greatest transition of my life. I was in a deep travail, a holy longing that I honestly cannot describe with human words. In that place, all I wanted to do was be close to God, to be known by God. It is not enough for me to know God; I must be intimately known by Him. He must be able to trust me. He must be able to share all of His secrets with me. I wanted Him to know that I was there for Him and cared about what was on His heart. Eventually, I realized I wasn't waiting on God, but He was waiting on me to live out on earth what was already written about me in His book in heaven. I'm part of His story because I'm His friend.

That thought transformed my life. I began to trust Him in ways I hadn't before. At times I felt super low and completely inadequate to do anything for the Lord, and despite me, as I prayed, He would use me mightily anyway. When these things happened, I realized how insignificant and small I really am compared to how wonderful, powerful, and awesome the Lord of all truly is. I realized the whole purpose of this entire book can be summed up in one phrase: *I want to be a friend of God.* Everything in the waiting season prepares us to be His friend. This book isn't just about telling you my stories, but about changing your perspective while you wait with God.

In my dream, I knew the book's last chapter would be a song title, but I didn't yet know how that fit. One day, I called my friend, Kasey Fuller, and she asked how my book was coming along. I told her it was going well and then shared the dream with her. After I shared the dream with her, I rambled on for quite a while about how the Lord had taken me to a deeper place with Him where I realized that nothing mattered except being a friend of God.

Then she said, "Oh, like the song, 'A Friend of God.'"

I was immediately blown away because I'd already titled the last chapter of my book, *"A Friend of God,"* even though I didn't realize it was a song title. That moment showed me that dreams really do come true.

COMING OUT OF THE WAITING

My waiting season was so long that I often wondered if I'd ever see the promised land or if the prophecies would actually come to pass. But something inside my spirit told me to keep believing and pressing forward to the other side. This book is a pivotal point in my life, a mile marker, as I cross over to the promised land. The waiting season isn't about just getting to the promised land, as if we leave the waiting and get into the promised land and all is well. It's about going from glory to glory. God always has more growth and maturation for us.

As I wrote this book, the direction it took looked quite different than the map I'd previously laid out. It felt like the Holy Spirit ministered to me through the writing of this book. I received a greater measure of His presence and anointing while writing, and He showed me many things I had not yet seen about my life. It was like watching a movie, and seeing into the unseen realm at the same time. I could see from the perspective of God instead of my perspective or the perspective of others. Through writing this book, I gained a more excellent knowledge of who Christ was, who He is, and who He will forever be. I pray you gained the same knowledge as well. I pray the anointing and presence of God floods you, overtakes you, and overwhelms you. I pray you'll never be the same, but will be forever changed into His image. I pray my journey in the waiting, the essence of my reality, will bless you and intertwine with your spirituality.

NOTES

4. THE GREAT STRIPPING AWAY

1. Kenneth E. Hagin, Hagin , K. E. (2013). *Bible Prayer Study Course* (Kindle Edition). Faith Library Publications.
2. Kathryn Kuhlman, Leaders, C. (2023, September 3). *10 marvelous Kathryn Kuhlman quotes*. Viral Believer. https://viralbeliever.com/kathryn-kuhlman-quotes/
3. Smith Wigglesworth, *Smith Wigglesworth - Real faith built the Ark, but real faith did not...* Read & Study the Bible Online – Bible Portal.(n.d.). https://bibleportal.com
4. Aimee Semple McPherson, *Top 8 quotes by Aimee Semple McPherson: A-Z quotes*. A. (n.d.). https://www.azquotes.com/author/21412-Aimee_Semple_McPherson
5. Derek Prince, *The importance of personal testimony: Podcast: Derek Prince Ministries.* Podcast | Derek Prince Ministries. (n.d.). https://www.derekprince.com/radio/536

6. DEEPER STILL

1. Dictionary.com. (n.d.). Decree definition & usage examples. Dictionary.com. https://www.dictionary.com/browse/decree#

7. PROPHETIC PUZZLES

1. Merriam-Webster. (n.d.). Testimony definition & meaning. Merriam-Webster. https://www.merriam-webster.com/dictionary/testimony#:~:text=1,authentica-tion%20of%20a%20fact%20%3A%20evidence

10. CONSIDER IT ALL JOY WHEN YOU FACE TRIALS

1. Destiny Image Pub. Shippensburg, PA (2016). The Key To True Life: Being Dead To Self. *Smith Wigglesworth on manifesting the power of god walking in god's anointing every day of the year* (pp. 66–68).

ABOUT THE AUTHOR

Cher Butler is a daughter of God, wife, and mother. In addition, she is the President of the I Will Not Keep Silent (IWNKS) Ministries, Founder of the Bound No More Deliverance Ministry, Co-Founder and Partner of the 333 Apostolic Center in Amarillo, Texas, and Co-Host of the Are You Real Podcast. She's also been a frequent guest on God's Learning Channel (GLC TV). She's been appointed for such a time as this and she runs with the torch of Christ in hand. She's been equipped by the POWER of Holy Spirit to serve the body of Christ. She's an apostolic ministry leader that trains and equips leaders in ministry and the marketplace. Furthermore, she's an entrepreneur, author, mentor, speaker, revivalist, teacher, prophetic seer, deliverance minister, and an aspiring innovator. She's a lover of Jesus Christ, and a glory carrier on a mission to spread the gospel.

https://www.iwnks.com

ABOUT THE CO-AUTHOR

Ruthie Dickey is the Co-Founder and Vice President of I Will Not Keep Silent Ministries, Co-Founder of Bound No More Deliverance Ministries, and Co-Founder of the 333 Apostolic Center. She was called by the father as a young adult but the enemy came in like a flood and tried to take her out. She was miraculously healed on her death bed through deliverance. She is a walking sign and wonder. She operates in the gifts of prophecy, words of knowledge and wisdom, healing, and a strong gift of distinguishing of spirits. She is a mentor, teacher, speaker, revivalist, and inner healing and deliverance minister. She's a retired social worker with 25+ years of experience. She has a heart for the broken and is able to pull out the gold that God planted in others.

Made in the USA
Columbia, SC
03 July 2024

38056512R00104